WAY TO THE QUR'ĀN

KHURRAM MURAD

THE ISLAMIC FOUNDATION

Published by

THE ISLAMIC FOUNDATION,

Markfield Conference Centre,
Ratby Lane, Markfield, Leicestershire
LE67 9SY, United Kingdom
E-mail: publications@islamic-foundation.com
Website: www.islamic-foundation.com

Quran House, PO Box 30611, Nairobi, Kenya

PMB 3193, Kano, Nigeria

Distributed by: Kube Publishing Ltd.
Tel: 44(01530) 249230, Fax: 44(01530) 249656
E-mail: info@kubepublishing.com

British Library Cataloguing-in-Publication Data
Murad, Khurram,
Way to the Qur'ān
1. Koran - Study
I. Title II. Islamic Foundation (Great Britain)
297'.122'07 BP130.8

ISBN: 978-0-86037-153-3

Cover design: Rashid Rahman

Printed by Imak Ofset - Turkey

بِسْمِ ٱللَّهِ ٱلرَّحْمَٰنِ ٱلرَّحِيمِ

أَنِ ٱشْكُرْ لِى وَلِوَٰلِدَيْكَ

'Be thankful to Me, and to your parents'
(Luqmān 31: 14)

to

MY MOTHER

At her knees I learnt to read the Qur'ān, upon her insistance that I must learn Arabic I was sent to the school *maulavi saheb* who gave me the rudimentary knowledge upon which I could build later; seeing her devotion to the Qur'ān, reading it with understanding, for hours and hours, kindled a spark in my heart which has continued to illumine my way; and, finally, through her example and silent but solid support I found my way to a life of struggle in the way of Allah.

'My Lord! Bestow Thy mercy upon my parents, as they
raised me up when I was little'
(al-Isrā' 17: 24)

Transliteration Table

Consonants. Arabic

initial: unexpressed medial and final:

ء	’	د	d	ض	ḍ	ك	k
ب	b	ذ	dh	ط	ṭ	ل	l
ت	t	ر	r	ظ	ẓ	م	m
ث	th	ز	z	ع	‘	ن	n
ج	j	س	s	غ	gh	هـ	h
ح	ḥ	ش	sh	ف	f	و	w
خ	kh	ص	ṣ	ق	q	ي	y

Vowels, diphthongs, etc.

Short:	ـَ	a	ـِ	i	ـُ	u
long:	ـَا	ā	ـُو	ū	ـِي	ī
diphthongs:			ـَوْ	aw		
			ـَيْ	ay		

Contents

Preface

Weak in faith and obedience as I am, and unlearned, my first duty must be to confess my utter inadequacy to write this book. For, says Allah, *subḥānahū wa ta'ālā* 'Had We sent down this Qur'ān upon a mountain, you would have seen it humbled and torn asunder by the fear of God.' So how can any human being, let alone one so poor in knowledge and impure in spirit, presume to point the way to the majesty and mercy, the beauty and wisdom that is the Qur'ān? What emboldened me, however, was the persistent nudging of many friends who felt that what I had shared with them needed to be shared by many more. But the real strength and courage came from Allah's promise: 'Those who strive in Our cause for Our sake, surely We shall guide them in Our ways.' And the Prophet's words, blessings and peace be on him – 'Convey on my behalf even if it be one Ayah' and 'Best among you is the one who learns the Qur'ān and teaches it' – seemed to make it almost a duty to be coveted.

My aim in writing this book is very modest. This is not a work of erudite scholarship. I am no learned *mufassir,* nor am I writing for scholars. I am not presuming to teach and guide, for I have no pretensions to that office. I am writing for those ordinary, inexpert and unlearned seekers after the Qur'ān, especially the young men and women, who are struggling hard to fulfil their desire to understand, absorb and live the Qur'ān, as I am doing myself. I am writing for students about things which I am learning myself.

In this book, then, I write as one wayfarer to another, trying to share with him whatever I have found and grasped as useful as I have stumbled, with all my deficiencies, along the easy and rewarding road *to* and *through* the Qur'ān. I am sure that they, with their greater sincerity, devotion and competence, will improve greatly upon what I have presented here.

This book is the product of a long and still-continuing search. Its contents have been gathered over many years of reading. The beginning of this book goes back more than three decades when I had just begun my own struggle to live by the Qur'ān, and when I was given the duty of explaining how to study the Qur'ān to a group of similarly committed young students. Most of what I said then, I owed to a small number of sources: Ḥamīduddīn Farāhī's *Tafāsīri Farāhī;* Sayyid Mawdūdī's *Tafhīmul Qur'ān;* Amīn Aḥsan Islāḥī's *Tadabburi Qur'ān;* al-Ghazālī's *Iḥyā' 'Ulūm al-Dīn;* Shāh Walīullāh's *Ḥujjah-Allāh al-Bālighah* and *al-Fawz al-Kabīr fi Uṣūl al-Tafsīr,* and Suyūṭī's *al-Itqān fi 'Ulūm al-Qur'ān.* For all that this book contains, I continue to owe a debt of gratitude to them. And whilst I would like to acknowledge this, I must also point out that none of these authors are responsible for my own errors of understanding and presentation. The first opportunity to put my thoughts in writing arose in 1977 when I wrote a short introduction to Yusuf Ali's translation of the Qur'ān published by the Islamic Foundation – 'The Way to the Qur'ān'.

This book is born out of certain abiding convictions. And whilst they are all explained in the book, it is useful to recall and summarize some of them here:

First, our lives will remain meaningless and ruined unless they are guided by the Qur'ān, the word of God.

Second, the Qur'ān, being the eternal guidance given by the Ever-living God, is as relevant for *us, today,* as it was fourteen centuries ago, and will remain so forever.

Third, we almost have a right, in some sense and measure, to receive its blessings today as its first believers did; provided, of course, that we come to it and move in it in a manner that may entitle us to share its rich harvest.

Fourth, every Muslim has a duty to devote himself to reading, understanding and memorizing the Qur'ān.

Fifth, one must abandon oneself totally, in thought and deed, to whatever the Qur'ān has to offer. Any pride, arrogance, sense of self-sufficiency, reservation, or ingenuity that can mistakenly be read into it, is fatal to its understanding and would shut the door to its blessings.

Sixth, the path of the Qur'ān is the path of self-surrender, of practising what it tells you, even if one learns only one Ayah. One Ayah learnt and acted upon is better than a thousand which are explained beautifully but which do not impart any beauty to the reader's life. Obedience, after all, is the real key to understanding.

There are seven chapters. Each deals with a different aspect of the journey. The first, dwells on what the journey means to our lives; the second, on what provisions must be gathered inside our hearts and minds before setting out; the third, on what postures and actions of heart, mind, and body are necessary for the full involvement of the inner self; the fourth, on what rules should be followed in reading; the fifth, on why and how to understand; the sixth, on how to undertake collective study; and the seventh, on the essential need of offering our lives to the fulfilment of the Qur'ānic mission. What the Prophet, blessings and peace be on him, said about some specific parts of the Qur'ān is gathered in one appendix. Another suggests certain syllabuses for personal and collective study, which many may find useful. Some study aids are also included.

This is not a book which should be put away after one hurried reading, unless one does not like what it says, or one does not find it useful. Those who need such a book and find it useful will, I hope, find it necessary to take plenty of time over each part, and to read it again and again. To them I would like to say: make it serve as your companion all along.

Some things you will have to study carefully, some you will have to store in your memory, some you will need to refer to frequently. But only what you practise will be of value to you. What this book does is to demarcate the road and erect the necessary signposts which point the way, give guidance, caution, warn, or prohibit, as the need may be. Still you will have to equip yourself with a vehicle, put fuel in it, come on the road, and drive. Nothing in the book can substitute for your inner longing, will and determination, and persistent effort.

A special word about the warnings and cautions spread throughout the book, about accepting and using what has been said here. They are important. Always keep them in mind, whether you are trying to understand the Qur'ān on your own, or using the syllabuses, or acting upon any other thing.

I have placed great emphasis on the urgent need for personal endeavours by each Muslim to try to understand the Qur'ān. To me this is the most fundamental demand of the Qur'ān. I am, however, aware of the pitfalls on this road, and these I have tried to note. In this respect, I would like you always to keep before you the words attributed to Sayyidinā Abū Bakr: 'Which earth will bear me and which sky will protect me if I say anything by my personal opinion in interpreting the Qur'ān.' This has always had a great sobering and steadying effect on me: you, too, should profit by it.

We are living in a time when the need to centre our lives on the Qur'ān is most urgent and compelling. Without this we Muslims will never rediscover our selves, never give meaning to our existence, never find dignity in this world. More importantly, we will never please our Creator and Lord. Without the Qur'ān, mankind, too, will continue to slide towards the abyss of total extinction.

There is today a rapidly growing realization of this urgency among Muslims. The desire to understand the Qur'ān and live by it has become widespread. The tide of Islamic resurgence is both a product of and a stimulant to this awareness and desire.

During these crucial days, if this humble effort succeeds in kindling in some hearts the desire to set out on the journey of the Qur'ān, a life-journey, and if it serves as their companion, my labours will be amply rewarded. Though it will benefit me only if Allah pardons all my errors of intention and understanding and blesses this endeavour of the heart with His acceptance. To those who benefit from this book, my plea is: do not forget me in your prayers.

Leicester
15 Sha'bān 1405
6 May 1985

Khurram Murad

1

The Journey of Life

The Eternal, Living Reality

The Qur'ān is the word of the Ever-living God; it has been sent down to guide man for all times to come. No book can be like it. As you come to the Qur'ān, Allah speaks to you. To read the Qur'ān is to hear Him, even to converse with Him, and to walk in His ways. It is the encounter of life with the Life-giver. 'God – there is no god but He, the Ever-living, the Self-subsisting (by whom all subsist). He has sent down upon you the Book with the Truth ... as a guidance unto mankind ...' (Āl 'Imrān 3: 2-3).

For those who heard it for the first time from the lips of the Prophet, blessings and peace be on him, the Qur'ān was a living reality. They had absolutely no doubt that, through him, Allah was speaking to them. Their hearts and minds were therefore seized by it. Their eyes overflowed with tears and their bodies shivered. They found each word of it deeply relevant to their concerns and experiences, and integrated it fully into their lives. They were completely transformed by it both as individuals and as a corporate body – into a totally new, alive and life-giving entity. Those who grazed sheep, herded camels and traded petty merchandise became the leaders of mankind.

Today we have the same Qur'ān with us. Millions of copies of it are in circulation. Day and night, it is ceaselessly recited. In homes, in mosques, and from pulpits. Voluminous exegetical works exist expounding its meaning. Words pour out incessantly to explain its teachings and to exhort us to live by it. Yet eyes remain dry, hearts remain unmoved, minds remain untouched, lives remain unchanged. Ignominy and degradation appear to have become the lot of the followers of the Qur'ān. Why? Because we no longer read the Qur'ān as a living reality. It is a sacred book, but it tells us something of the past only, concerning Muslims and Kafirs, Jews and Christians, the faithful and the hypocrites, who 'once upon a time used to be'.

Can the Qur'ān, again, be a living, relevant force, as powerful for us now, 1400 years away, as it was then? This is the most crucial question that we must answer if we wish to shape our destiny afresh under the guidance of the Qur'ān.

There appear, however, to be some difficulties. Not least of which has to do with the fact that the Qur'ān was revealed at a certain point in time. Since then we have travelled a long way, made gigantic leaps in technological know-how, and seen considerable social changes take place in human society. Moreover, most of the followers of the Qur'ān today do not know Arabic, and many who do have little idea of the 'living' language of the Qur'ān. They cannot be expected to absorb its idiom and metaphor, so essential to exploring and absorbing the depths of the Qur'ānic meaning.

Yet its guidance, by its own claim, has an eternal relevance for all people, being the word of the Eternal God.

For the truth of this claim, it seems to me, it must be *possible* for us to receive, experience, and understand the Qur'ān as its first recipients did, at least in some measure and to some degree. We seem to almost have a right to this possibility of receiving God's guidance in its fullness and with all its riches and joys. In other words, despite the historical incidence of the revelation in a particular language at a particular time and place, we should be capable of receiving the Qur'ān *now* (because its message is eternal), capable of making its message as much a real part of our lives as it was for the first believers and with the same urgent and profound relevance for all our present concerns and experiences.

But how do we do this? To put it very forthrightly, only by entering the world of the Qur'ān as if Allah were speaking to us through it *now* and *today,* and by fulfilling the necessary conditions for such an encounter.

Firstly, then, we must realize what the Qur'ān as the word of God is and means to us, and bring all the reverence, love, longing, and will to act that this realization demands. *Secondly,* we must read it as it asks to be read, as Allah's Messenger instructed us, as he and his Companions read it. *Thirdly,* we must bring each word of the Qur'ān to bear upon our own realities and concerns by transcending the barriers of time, culture and change.

For its first addressees, the Qur'ān was a contemporary event. Its language and style, its eloquence and rationale, its idiom and metaphor, its symbols and parables, its moments and events were all rooted in their own setting. These people were both witnesses to and, in a sense, participants in the whole act of revelation as it unfolded over a period of their own time. We do not have the same privilege; yet, in some measure, the same ought to be true for us.

By understanding and obeying the Qur'ān in our own setting, we will find it, as far as possible, as much a contemporary event for ourselves as it was then. For the essence of man has not changed; it is immutable. Only man's externalities - the forms, the modes, the technologies - have changed. The pagans of Makka may be no more, nor the Jews of Yathrib, nor the Christians of Najran, nor even the 'faithful' and the 'unfaithful' of the community at Madina; but the same characters exist all around us. We are human beings exactly as the first recipients were, even though many find it extremely difficult to grapple with the deep implications of this very simple truth.

Once you realize these truths and follow them, once you come to the Qur'ān as the first believers did, it may reveal to you as it did to them, make partners of you as it did of them. And only then, instead of being a mere revered book, a sacred fossil, or a source of magic-like blessing, it will change into a mighty force, impinging, stirring, moving and guiding us to deeper and higher achievements, just as it did before.

The New World that Awaits You

As you come to the Qur'ān, you come to a new world. No other venture in your life can be so momentous and crucial, so blissful and rewarding, as your journey *to* and *through* the Qur'ān.

It is a journey that will take you through the endless joys and riches of the words that your Creator and Lord has sent to you and all mankind. Here you will find a world of untold treasures of knowledge and wisdom to guide you on the pathways of life, to mould your thoughts and actions. In it you will find deep insights to enrich you and steer you along the right course. From it you will receive a radiant light to illumine the deeper reaches of your soul. Here you will encounter profound emotions, a warmth to melt your heart and bring tears running down your cheeks.

It is crucial for you because, as you travel through the Qur'ān, at every step you will be summoned to choose, and to commit to Allah. To read the Qur'ān is nothing less than to live the Qur'ān willingly, sincerely, devotedly, and totally. The outcome of your entire life depends on how you heed the call given by God. The journey is therefore decisive for your existence, for mankind, for the future of human civilization.

> A hundred new worlds lie in its verses.
> Whole centuries are involved in its moments.*

---

*Muhammad Iqbal, *Javid Nama,* trans. A. J. Arberry (London, 1967).

Know, then, that it is the Qur'ān, and only the Qur'ān, which can lead you on and on to success and glory in *this*-world and in the world-to-come.

What is the Qur'ān?

It is beyond man's power to comprehend, or to describe, the greatness and importance of what the Qur'ān holds for him. Yet, to begin with, you must have some idea of what it is and what it means to you, such that you are inspired to immerse the whole of your self in the Qur'ān, in total commitment, complete dedication and ceaseless pursuit, as it demands.

The Qur'ān is Allah's greatest blessing for you. It is the fulfilment of His promise to Adam and his descendants: 'There shall come to you guidance from Me, and whosoever follows My guidance no fear shall be on them, neither shall they sorrow' (al-Baqarah 2: 38). It is the only weapon to help your frail existence as you struggle against the forces of evil and temptation in this-world. It is the only means to overpower your fear and anxiety. It is the only 'light' (*nūr*), as you grope in the darkness, with which to find your way to success and salvation. It is the only healing (*shifā'*) for your inner sicknesses, as well as the social ills that may surround you. It is the constant reminder (*dhikr*) of your true nature and destiny, of your station, your duties, your rewards, your perils.

It was brought down by one who is powerful and trustworthy in the heavens - the angel Jibra'īl. Its first abode was that pure and sublime heart, the like of which man has never had - the heart of the Prophet Muhammad, blessings and peace be on him.

More than anything, it is the only way to come nearer and closer to your Creator. It tells you of Him, of His attributes, of how He rules over the cosmos and history, of how He relates Himself to you, and how you should relate to Him, to yourself, to your fellow men and to every other existence.

The rewards that await you here are surely many, increasing manifold in the Hereafter, but what awaits you at the end of the road, promises Allah in the *Ḥadīth qudsī*, 'the eye has seen not, nor the ear heard, nor the heart of man ever conceived', and, adds Abū Hurayrah: read if you wish [in al-Sajdah 32: 17]: 'No human being can imagine what joys are being kept hidden for them in reward for all that they did' (*Bukhārī, Muslim*).

Infinite Mercy and Majesty

Most important to remember is that what you read in the Qur'ān is the word of Allah, the Lord of the worlds, which He has conveyed to you in a human language, only because of His mercy and care and providence for you. 'The Most-merciful, He has taught the Qur'ān' (al-Raḥmān 55: 1-2). 'A mercy from your Lord' (al-Dukhān 44: 6). The majesty of the Qur'ān, too, is so overpowering that no human being can comprehend it. So much so that, says Allah: 'If We had sent down this Qur'ān upon a mountain, you would have seen it humbled, split asunder out of the fear of Allah' (al-Ḥashr 59: 20).

This act of Divine mercy and majesty is enough to awe and overwhelm you, to inspire you to ever-greater heights of gratitude, yearning and endeavour to enter the world of the Qur'ān. Indeed, no treasure is more valuable and precious for you than the Qur'ān, as Allah says of His generosity:

> O men! There has come to you an exhortation from your Lord, healing for what is in the hearts, and a guidance, and a mercy for believers. Say: In [this] bounty of Allah, and in His mercy – in it let them rejoice. It is better than whatever they amass (Yūnus 10: 57-8).

Hazards and Perils

Rejoice you must, in the mercy and blessing and generosity of Allah. Seek you must, for the treasures that await your search herein. But the Qur'ān opens its doors only to those who knock with a sense of yearning, a sincerity of purpose and an exclusive attention that befit its importance and majesty. And only those are allowed to gather its treasures, while they walk through it, who are prepared to abandon themselves completely to its guidance and do their utmost to absorb it.

It may quite possibly happen therefore that you may read the Qur'ān endlessly, turn its pages laboriously, recite its words beautifully, study it most scholarly, and still fail to make an encounter with it that enriches and transforms your whole person. For, all those who read the Qur'ān do not profit from it as they should. Some remain unblessed; some are even cursed.

The journey has its own hazards, as it must, just as it has its own precious and limitless rewards. Many never turn to it, though the Book always lies near at hand, and many are turned away from its gates. Many read it often, but come back empty-handed; while many others who read it never really enter its world. Some do not *find*, but are *lost.* They fail to hear God even among His own words; instead, they hear their own voices or those other than God's. Still others, though they hear God, fail to find inside themselves the will, the resolve and the courage to respond and live by His call. Some lose even what they had and, instead of collecting priceless gems, they return with back-breaking loads of stones which will hurt them for ever and ever.

What a tragic misfortune it would be if you came to the Qur'ān and went away empty-handed - soul untouched, heart unmoved, life unchanged; 'they went out as they came in'.

The Qur'ān's blessings are limitless, but the measure of your taking from it depends entirely upon the capacity and the suitability of the receptacle you bring to it. So, at the very outset, make yourself more deeply aware of what the Qur'ān means to you and what it demands of you; and make a solemn determination to recite the Qur'ān in an appropriate manner, so that you may be counted among 'Those whom We have given the Book, they recite it as it ought to be recited; it is they who believe in it' (al-Baqarah 2: 121).

Tilāwah

Tilāwah is the word that the Qur'ān uses to describe the act of its reading. No single word in English can convey its full meaning. 'To follow' is closest to its primary meaning. To read is only secondary, for in reading too, words follow each other, one closely behind the other, in an orderly and meaningful sequence. If one word does not follow the other, or if the sequence and order is not observed, the meaning is destroyed.

So, primarily, *tilāwah* means to move closely behind, to go forward, to flow in a sequence, to go in pursuit, to take as a guide, leader, master, a model, to accept the authority, to espouse the cause, to act upon, walk after, practise a way of life, to understand, to follow the train of thought - *or* to follow. Reading the Qur'ān, understanding the Qur'ān, following the Qur'ān - that is how those who have any right to claim faith in it relate themselves to it.

Tilāwah or recitation is an act in which your whole person - soul, heart, mind, tongue and body - participates. In short your whole existence becomes involved. In reading the Qur'ān, mind and body, reason and feeling lose their distinction; they become fused. As the tongue recites and words flow from the lips, the mind ponders, the heart reflects, the soul absorbs, tears well up in the eyes, the heart quakes and trembles, the skin shivers and softens just as the heart does, there no longer remains any duality between the two, even your hair may stand on end. And 'so he walks in a light from his

Lord ... that is God's guidance, whereby He guides whomsoever He will' (al-Zumar 39: 22-3).

To read the Qur'ān thus, as it deserves to be read, is not a light task; but nor is it too difficult or impossible. Otherwise the Qur'ān could not have been meant for laymen like us, nor could it be the mercy and the guidance that it surely is. But obviously it does entail much travail of heart and mind, soul and intellect, spirit and body, and requires that certain conditions be observed and obligations be fulfilled – some inwardly, some outwardly. You should know them all, now, and endeavour to observe them before you enter the glorious world of the Qur'ān.

Only then will you reap the full harvest of blessings that await you in the Qur'ān. Only then will the Qur'ān open its doors to you. Only then will it let you dwell inside it and dwell inside you. Nine months spent in the womb of your mother have transformed a drop of water into 'you' – hearing, seeing and thinking. Can you imagine what a lifetime spent with the Qur'ān – seeking, hearing, seeing, thinking, striving – can do for you? It can make you into an entirely new 'being' – before whom even angels will feel proud to kneel.

Ascending at every step taken within the Qur'ān and every moment spent therein, you will reach towering heights. You will be gripped by the power and beauty that breathe and move within the Qur'ān.

> From 'Abdullāh ibn 'Amr ibn al-'Āṣ: The Prophet, Allah's blessings and peace be on him, said, 'The companion of the Qur'ān will be told: recite and ascend, ascend with facility as you used to recite with facility in the world. Your final abode is the height you reach at the last verse you recite.' (*Abū Dā'ūd, Tirmidhī, Aḥmad, Nasā'ī*)

2

Basic Prerequisites

Certain basic states and attitudes of heart and mind are a necessary prerequisite to any fruitful relationship with the Qur'ān. Develop them as much as you can. Make them part of your consciousness, keep them ever-alive and active. Integrate them in your actions. Let them penetrate the depth of your being. Without the help of these inner resources you will not receive your full measure of the Qur'ān's blessings. They will be your indispensable companions, too, throughout your journey.

These inner resources are neither difficult nor impossible to find. Through constant awareness and reflection, through appropriate words and deeds, you can acquire and develop them. The more you do so, the closer you will be able to come to the Qur'ān; the closer you come to the Qur'ān, the greater will be your harvest.

Faith: The Word of God

First: Come to the Qur'ān with a strong and deep faith that it is the word of Allah, your Creator and Lord.

Why should such a faith be a necessary prerequisite? No doubt such is the power and charm of the Qur'ān that even if a man takes it up and starts reading it as he would an ordinary book, he will still benefit from it, should he read it with an open mind. But this Book is no ordinary book; it opens with the emphatic statement:

'This is the Book [of God], there is no doubt in it' (al-Baqarah 2: 2). Your purpose in reading and studying it is no ordinary purpose; you seek from it the guidance that will transform your whole being, bring you and keep you on the Straight Path: 'Guide us on the Straight Path' (al-Fātiḥah 1: 5) is the cry of your heart to which the Qur'ān is the response.

You may admire the Qur'ān, even be informed by it, but you cannot be transformed by it unless its words soak in to awaken you, to grip you, to heal and change you. This cannot happen unless you take them for what they truly are - the words of God.

Without this faith you cannot come to acquire all the other inner resources you will need to reach the heart of the Qur'ān and absorb its message. Once it comes to reside in your heart, you cannot but be filled with the qualities and attitudes such as sincerity of purpose, awe and reverence, love and gratitude, trust and dependence, willingness to labour hard, conviction of its truth, surrender to its message, obedience to its commands, and vigilance against dangers which stalk to deprive you of its treasures.

Think of His majesty and glory and power, and you will feel awe and reverence and devotion for His words. Reflect on His sustenance and mercy and compassion, and you will be filled with gratitude and love and longing for His message. Know His wisdom and knowledge and kindness, and you will become willing and eager and ready to obey His commandments.

That is why the Qur'ān reminds you of this important truth again and again: in the very beginning, in the opening verses of many Surahs, and frequently in between.

That is why even the Messenger, blessings and peace be on him, is instructed to proclaim his own faith: 'Say: I believe in whatever God has sent down in this Book' (al-Shūrā 42: 15). In his faith all believers must join him: 'The Messenger believes in what has been sent down to him by His Lord, and all believers too' (al-Baqarah 2: 285).

You must, therefore, always remain conscious that each word that you are reading, reciting, hearing, or trying to understand, has been sent for you by Allah.

Do you truly have this faith? You do not have to look far for an answer. Just examine your heart and behaviour. If you have it, then, where is the desire and longing for companionship with the Qur'ān, where is the labour and hard work to understand it, where is the surrender and obedience to its message?

How do we obtain this faith, and how can it be kept alive? Although there are many ways, I will mention only one here. The most effective way is reciting the Qur'ān itself. This may look as if we are moving in a circle, but this is not really the case. For, as you read the Qur'ān, you will surely recognize it as being the word of God. Your faith will then increase in intensity and depth:

> Believers are only those who, whenever God is mentioned, their hearts tremble with awe; and whenever His revelations are recited to them, they increase them in faith ... (al-Anfāl 8: 2).

Purity of Intention and Purpose

Second: Read the Qur'ān with no purpose other than to receive guidance from your Lord, to come nearer to Him, and to seek His good pleasure.

What you get from the Qur'ān depends on what you come to it for. Your *niyyah* (intention and purpose) is crucial. Certainly the Qur'ān has come to guide you, but you may also go astray by reading it should you approach it for impure purposes and wrong motives.

> Thereby He causes many to go astray, and thereby He guides many; but thereby He causes none to go astray save the iniquitous (al-Baqarah 2: 26).

The Qur'ān is the word of Allah; it therefore requires as much exclusiveness of intention and purity of purpose as does worshipping and serving Him.

Do not read it merely for intellectual pursuit and pleasure; even though you must apply your intellect to the full to the task of understanding the Qur'ān. So many people spend a lifetime in studying the language, style, history, geography, law and ethics of the Qur'ān, and yet their lives remain untouched by its message. The Qur'ān frequently refers to people who have knowledge but do not derive benefit from it.

Nor should you come to the Qur'ān with the fixed intention of finding support for your own views, notions and doctrines. For if you do, you may, then, hear an echo of your own voice in it, and not that of God. It is this approach to the understanding and interpreting of the Qur'ān that the Prophet, blessings and peace be on him, has condemned. 'Whoever interprets the Qur'ān by his personal opinion shall take his place in the Fire' (*Tirmidhī*).

Nothing could be more unfortunate than to use the Qur'ān to secure, for your own person, worldly things such as name, esteem, status, fame or money. You may get them, but you will surely be bartering away a priceless treasure for nothing, indeed even incurring eternal loss and ruin. Indeed, the Prophet, blessings and peace be on him, said: 'If anyone studies the Qur'ān seeking thereby a living from people, he will rise on the Day of Resurrection with his face as a fleshless bone' (*Bayhaqī*). He also said that one who learns, recites and teaches the Qur'ān for worldly acclaim will be thrown into the Fire (*Muslim*).

You may also derive other lesser benefits, from the words of the Qur'ān, such as the healing of bodily afflictions, psychological peace, and deliverance from poverty. There is no bar to having these, but, again, they should not become the *be all and end all* that you seek from the Qur'ān nor the goal of your *niyyah*. For in achieving these you may lose a whole ocean that could have been yours.

Reading every single letter of the Qur'ān carries with it great rewards. Remain conscious of all the rewards, and make them an objective of your *niyyah*, for they will provide you with those strong incentives required to spend your life with the Qur'ān. But never forget that on understanding, absorbing and following the Qur'ān you have been promised much larger rewards, in this-world and in the Hereafter. It is these which you must aim for.

Not only should your purpose be pure, but you should also, once you have the Qur'ān with you - both the text and its living embodiment in the Sunnah - never go to any other source for guidance. For that would be like running after mirages. It would mean a lack of confidence, a denigration of the Qur'ān. It would amount to divided loyalties.

Nothing brings you nearer to your Lord than the moments you spend with His words. For it is only in the Qur'ān that you enjoy the unique blessing of hearing His 'voice' addressing you. So let an intense desire to come nearer to Allah be your one overwhelming motive while reading the Qur'ān.

Finally, your *niyyah* should be directed to seeking only your Lord's pleasure by devoting your heart, mind and time to the guidance that He has sent to you. That is what you barter when you surrender yourself to Allah: 'There is such as would sell his own self in order to please God' (al-Baqarah 2: 207).

Purpose and intentions are like the soul of a body, the inner capability of a seed. Many seeds look alike, but as they begin to grow and bear fruits, their differences become manifest. The purer and higher the motive, the greater the value and yield of your efforts.

So always ask yourself: Why am I reading the Qur'ān? Tell yourself constantly why you should. This may be the best way to ensure the purity and exclusiveness of purpose and intention.

Bringing Gratitude and Praise

Third: Make yourself constantly alert with intense praise and gratitude to your Lord for having blessed you with His greatest gift – the Qur'ān – and for having guided you to its reading and study.

Once you realize what a priceless treasure you hold in your hands, it is but natural for your heart to beat with joy and murmur, and for your tongue to join in: 'Thankful praise be to Allah, who has guided us to this; [otherwise] never could we have found guidance had not Allah not guided us' (al-A'rāf 7: 43).

Of all the intimate blessings and favours He has bestowed upon you nothing can match the Qur'ān. If every hair on your body becomes a tongue praising and thanking Him, if every drop of blood in your body turns into a joyful tear, even then your praise and thanks will not match His enormous generosity that is the Qur'ān.

Even if the Qur'ān had not been sent down *for* us, its perfection and beauty, its majesty and splendour would deserve all the praise at our command. But that this sublime and perfect gift, having the unique distinction of embodying our Lord's speech, has been given solely for our sake must intensify our praise beyond bounds.

Such intense praise inevitably turns into intense gratitude. And no word expresses this intense praise combined with overflowing gratitude and thanks as well as does *al-ḥamd.*

alḥamdu li 'llāhi 'l-ladhī hadāna li hādhā ...

Why thank Allah for having given us the Qur'ān? Principally because He has, thus, guided you to meaning and purpose in life and brought you on the Straight Path. The way to honour and dignity in this-world has been opened for you. In the Qur'ān, you can converse with Allah. Only by following the Qur'ān in this-world can you attain forgiveness, Paradise and Allah's good pleasure in that-world.

Gratitude and joy lead to trust, hope and greater gifts. The One who has given you the Qur'ān will surely help you in reading, understanding and following it. Thankfulness and joy generate an ever-fresh vigour which helps you to read the Qur'ān always with a renewed zeal. The more you are grateful, the more Allah gives you of the riches that the Qur'ān has to offer. Generosity evokes gratitude, gratitude makes you deserve more generosity – an unending cycle. Such is God's promise: 'If you are grateful, I will surely give you more and more' (Ibrāhīm 14: 7).

Having the Qur'ān and not feeling immensely grateful for it can only mean two things: either you are ignorant of the blessings that the Qur'ān contains, or you do not attach any importance to them. In either case you should be seriously worried about the state of your relationship with the Qur'ān.

The sentiment of gratitude that permeates every pore of your heart and mind, must also pour out in your words, which should be profuse and incessant. Thank Allah at every step of your journey: for having had time for the Qur'ān, for reading it correctly, for memorizing it, for every meaning you discover in it, for having been enabled to follow it. Gratitude must also be transformed into deeds.

Acceptance and Trust

Fourth: Accept and trust, without the least doubt or hesitation, every knowledge and guidance that the Qur'ān conveys to you.

You have the freedom to question whether the Qur'ān is the word of Allah or not, and to reject its claim if you are not satisfied. But once you have accepted it as His word, you have no basis whatever to doubt even a single word of it. For to do so would negate what you have accepted. There must be total surrender and abandonment to the Qur'ānic teachings. Your own beliefs, opinions, judgements, notions, whims should not be allowed to override any part of it.

The Qur'ān condemns those who receive the Book as an inheritance and then behave as bewildered and puzzled, doubting and sceptical 'believers'.

> Those whom the Book has been given as an inheritance after them [the early people], behold they are in doubt about it, disquieting (al-Shūrā 42: 14).

The Qur'ān also repeatedly emphasizes that every measure was taken to ensure that it came down and was conveyed without any adulteration.* And affirms:

> With the Truth We have sent it down and with the Truth it has come down (al-Isrā' 17: 105).
>
> And perfect are the words of your Lord in Truth and Justice (al-An'ām 6: 115).

Accepting and trusting the Qur'ān as true, and wholly true, does not mean blind faith, closed minds, unenquiring intellects.

You have every right to enquire, reflect, question and understand what it contains; but what you cannot fully comprehend is not necessarily irrational or untrue. In a mine where you believe that every stone is a priceless gem - and it may have proved to be so - you will not throw away the few whose worth your eyes fail to detect or which the tools available to you are inadequate or unable to evaluate.

Nor can part of the Qur'ān be discarded as being out of date and old-fashioned, an old wives' tale. If God is Lord of all times, His message must be equally valid fourteen centuries later.

To accept some part of the Qur'ān and to reject some is to reject all of it. There is no room for partial acceptance in your relationship with the Qur'ān; there cannot logically be (al-Baqarah 2: 85).

---

* al-Burūj 85: 21; al-Takwīr 81: 19-21; 'Abasa 80: 15-16; Fuṣṣilat 41: 41-2.

There are many diseases of the heart and mind which may prevent you from accepting the Qur'ānic message and surrendering to it. They have all been described in the Qur'ān. Among them are envy, prejudice, gratification of one's desires and the blind following of the ways and customs of society. But the greatest are pride and arrogance, a sense of self-sufficiency (*kibr* and *istighnā'*) which prevent you from giving up your own opinions, recognizing the word of God, and accepting it with humility.

> I shall turn away from My revelations all those who wax proud in the earth, without any right; though they see every sign, they do not believe in it, and though they see the way of rectitude, they do not take it for a way, and if they see the way of error, they take it for a way (al-A'rāf 7: 146).

> And those who deny Our revelations and wax proud against them – the gates of heaven shall not be opened to them, nor shall they enter Paradise until a camel passes through a needle's eye (al-A'rāf 7: 40).

Obedience and Change

Fifth: Bring the will, resolve and readiness to obey whatever the Qur'ān says, and change your life, attitudes and behaviour – inwardly and outwardly – as desired by it.

Unless you are prepared and begin to act to shape your thoughts and actions according to the messages you receive from the Qur'ān, all your dedication and labour may be to no avail. Mere intellectual exercises and ecstatic experiences will never bring you anywhere near the real treasures of the Qur'ān.

Failing to obey the Qur'ān and to change your life because of human frailties and temptations, natural difficulties and external impediments is one matter; failing to do so because you have no intention or make no effort to do so is quite another. You may, then attain fame as a scholar of the Qur'ān, but it will never reveal its true meaning to you.

The Qur'ān reserves one of its most severe condemnations for those who profess faith in the Book of God, but when they are summoned to act or when situations arise for decision-making, they ignore its call or turn away from it. They have been declared to be *Kāfir*, *fāsiq* (iniquitous), *ẓālim* (wrongdoer).

Hazards and Obstacles

Sixth: Always remain aware that, as you embark upon reading the Qur'ān, Satan will create every possible hazard and obstacle to stalk you on your way to the great riches of the Qur'ān.

The Qur'ān is the only sure guide to the Straight Path to God; to walk that path is man's destiny. When Adam was created he was made aware of the hurdles and obstacles man would have to surmount in order to fulfil his destiny. All his weaknesses were laid bare, especially his weakness of will and resolve and his forgetfulness (Ṭā Hā 20: 115). It was also made plain how Satan would try to obstruct him at every step of his journey:

> I shall surely sit in ambush for them all along Thy Straight Path; I shall, then, come on them from between their hands and from behind them, from their right and their left. Thou wilt not find most of them thankful (al-A'rāf 7: 16-17).

Obviously the Qur'ān – the 'Guidance from Me' – is your most powerful ally and help as you battle all your life against Satan and strive to live by God's guidance. Hence, from the very first step when you decide to read the Qur'ān till the last when you try to live by it, he will confront you with many tricks and guiles, illusions and deceptions, obstacles and impediments which you will have to surmount.

Satan may pollute your intention, make you remain unmindful of the Qur'ān's meaning and message, create doubts in your mind, erect barriers between your soul and the world of Allah, entangle you in peripheral rather than central teachings, tempt you away from obeying the Qur'ān, or simply make you neglect and postpone the task of reading it. All of these dangers are fully explained in the Qur'ān itself.

Take just one very simple thing. Reading the Qur'ān every day, while understanding it, sounds very easy. But try, and you will find how difficult it becomes: time slips away, other important things come up. Concentrating mind and attention become something you wish to avoid: why not just read quickly for *barakah.*

It is with the consciousness of these perils and dangers that your tongue should, in obedience to the Qur'ān – 'When you recite the Qur'ān, seek refuge with Allah from Satan, the rejected' (al-Naḥl 16: 98) – say:

a'ūdhu billāhi mina 'sh-Shayṭāni 'r-rajīm

Trust and Dependence

Seventh: Trust, exclusively and totally, in Allah to lead you to the full rewards of reading the Qur'ān.

Just as it has been Allah's infinite mercy that has brought His words to you in the Qur'ān and brought you to it, so it can be only His mercy that can help in your crucial task. You need weighty and precious provisions, and these are not easy to procure. You face immense dangers, which are difficult to overcome. Whom can you look to but Him to hold you by the hand and guide you on your way.

Your desire and effort are the necessary means; but His enabling grace and support are the only sure guarantees that you will be able to tread your way with success and profit. In Him alone you should trust as true believers. To Him alone you must turn for everything in life. And what thing is more important than the Qur'ān?

Also, never be proud of what you are doing for the Qur'ān, of what you have achieved. Always be conscious of your inadequacies and limitations in the face of a task which has no parallel.

So approach the Qur'ān with humility, with a sense of utter dependence upon Allah, seeking His help and support at every step.

It is in this spirit of trust, praise and gratitude, that you should let your tongue and heart, in mutual harmony, begin the recitation:

> *Bismi 'llāhi 'r-Raḥmāni 'r-Raḥīm*
>
> In the name of Allah, the Most-merciful, the Mercy- giving

This is the verse which appears at the head of all but one of the 114 Surahs of the Qur'ān. And also pray, asking His protection:

> Our Lord! Let not our hearts swerve [from the Truth] after Thou hast guided us; and bestow upon us Thy mercy, indeed Thou alone art the Bestower (Āl 'Imrān 3: 8).

3

Participation of the Inner Self

Reading the Qur'ān, the *tilāwah*, must involve your whole 'person'. Only thus will you be able to elevate your encounter with the Qur'ān to the level where you can be called a 'true' believer in the Qur'ān (al-Baqarah 2: 121).

What is the Heart?

The more important part of your 'person' is your inner self. This inner self the Qur'ān calls the *qalb* or the 'heart'. The heart of the Prophet, blessings and peace be on him, was the first recipient of the Qur'ānic message:

> Truly it has been sent down by the Lord of all the worlds, the Trustworthy Spirit has alighted with it upon your heart [O Prophet], that you may be one of the warners ... (al-Shu'arā' 26: 192-4).

You will therefore reap the full joys and blessings of reading the Qur'ān when you are able to involve your heart fully in your task.

The 'heart', in Qur'ānic vocabulary, is not the piece of flesh in your body, but the centre of all your feelings, emotions, motives, drives, aspirations, remembrance and attention. It is the hearts which soften (al-Zumar 39: 23), or harden and become stony (al-Baqarah 2: 74). It is they which go blind and refuse to recognize the truth (al-Ḥajj 22: 46) for it is their function to reason and understand (al-A'rāf 7: 179; al-Ḥajj 22: 46; Qāf 50: 37). In hearts, lie the roots of all outward diseases (al-Mā'idah 5: 52); they are the seat of all inner ills (al-Baqarah 2: 10); hearts are the abode of Īmān (al-Mā'idah 5: 41) and hypocrisy (al-Tawbah 9: 77). It is the hearts, again, which are the centre of every good and bad thing, whether it be contentment and peace (al-Ra'd 13: 28), the strength to face afflictions (al-Taghābun 64: 11), mercy (al-Ḥadīd 57: 27), brotherly love (al-Anfāl 8: 63), *taqwā* (al-Ḥujurāt 49: 3; al-Ḥajj 22: 32); or, doubt and hesitation (al-Tawbah 9: 45), regrets (Āl 'Imrān 3: 156), and anger (al-Tawbah 9: 15). Finally it is, in reality, the ways of the heart for which we shall be accountable, and only the one who brings before his God a sound and whole heart will deserve to be saved.

> God will not take you to task for a slip, but He will take you to task for what your hearts have earned (al-Baqarah 2: 225).
>
> The Day when neither wealth nor children shall profit, [and when] only he [will be saved] who comes before God with a sound heart [free of evil] (al-Shu'arā' 26: 88-9).

You must therefore ensure that so long as you are with the Qur'ān, your heart remains with you. The heart not being that piece of flesh but what the Qur'ān calls *qalb*.

This should not prove difficult if you remain conscious of a few things and observe certain actions of heart and body. The seven prerequisites described earlier lay the foundation for the fuller participation of your inner self in reading the Qur'ān. In addition to these, the taking of a few more steps will greatly increase the intensity and quality of this involvement of the heart.

Dynamic of Inner Participation

You should understand the dynamic of inner participation well. For how is your heart seized by Truth? *First,* you come to know the truth. *Second,* you recognize and accept it as the truth and as relevant to your life. *Third,* you remember the truth, as much and as often as you can. *Fourth,* you absorb it until it soaks into the deepest recesses of your inner self. The truth thus becomes an ever-alive state of consciousness, an enduring posture of the heart. Once a truth so permeates your inner world, it must pour out in the world of words and deeds.

It is also important to remember here that what you do outwardly, by your tongue and limbs, interacts with what you are inwardly. It is possible that words and deeds may be false witnesses to the state of inner self. But an inner state, like faith, must necessarily find expression in words and deeds, which, in turn, must help in engraving your knowledge in your consciousness and turn it into an abiding condition.

The steps suggested here will be effective if you remain mindful of the above dynamics and follow the above principles.

States of Consciousness

There are seven states of consciousness which you must try to develop by remembering certain things, absorbing them and by frequently reminding yourself of them.

The Qur'ānic Criteria of Inner Participation

First: Say to yourself: My Qur'ān reading will not be truly *tilāwah* unless my inner self participates in it as Allah desires it to participate.

So what does Allah desire? And how should you receive the Qur'ān? The Qur'ān itself in many places tells you vividly how it was received by the Prophet, blessings and peace be on him, and by his Companions, and by those whose hearts were gripped by it. Such Qur'ānic verses you should try to remember, and, then, recollect and reflect upon them whenever you read the Qur'ān. Some of these are:

> Those only are believers who, when Allah is mentioned, their hearts tremble; and when His verses are recited to them, they increase them in faith (al-Anfāl 8: 2).
>
> God has sent down the best discourse as a Book, fully consistent within itself, oft-repeated, whereat shiver the skins of those who fear their Lord; then their skins and hearts soften to the remembrance of Allah (al-Zumar 39: 23).
>
> When it is recited to them, they fall down upon their faces, prostrating, and say: Glory be to our Lord! Our Lord's promise is fulfilled. And they fall down upon their faces, weeping; and it increases them in humility (al-Isrā' 17: 107-9).
>
> Whenever the verses of the Most-merciful are read unto them, they fall down, prostrating themselves and weeping (Maryam 19: 58).
>
> And when they hear what has been sent down to the Messenger, you see their eyes overflow with tears because of what they have recognized of Truth. They cry: Our Lord! We believe; so You do write us down among the witnesses [to the Truth] (al-Mā'idah 5: 83).

In Allah's Presence

Second: Say to yourself: I am in Allah's presence; He is seeing me.

You must remain alive to the reality that, while you are reading the Qur'ān, you are in the very presence of Him who has sent these words to you. For, Allah is always with you, wherever you are, whatever you are doing. His knowledge is all-encompassing.

How do you attain this state of consciousness? Listen to what Allah tells you in the Qur'ān in this regard. Remember those verses, and recollect and reflect upon them when you are about to start reading the Qur'ān, and during it. But what will help you more, not only in reading the Qur'ān but in living your whole life by the Qur'ān, is to remember and reflect this reality as often as you can. Alone or in company, silent or speaking, at home or at work, at rest or busy - say, silently or loudly: He is here, with me, seeing and hearing, knowing and recording. And remember these verses of the Qur'ān:

> He is with you wherever you are (al-Ḥadīd 57: 4).
> We are nearer to him than his jugular vein (Qāf 50: 16).
>
> Three men converse not secretly together, but He is the fourth of them, neither five men, but He is the sixth of them, neither fewer than that, neither more, but He is with them, wherever they may be (al-Mujādalah 58: 7)
>
> I am with you two [Mūsā and Hārūn], hearing and seeing (Ṭā Hā 20: 46).
>
> Surely you are before Our eyes (al-Ṭūr 52: 48).
>
> Surely it is We who bring the dead to life and write down what they have sent ahead and what they have left behind, everything We have taken into account in a clear register (Yā Sīn 36: 12).

More significant is the following verse, which not only forcefully tells, in general, about Allah being present everywhere, seeing everything, but mentions, specifically, the act of reading the Qur'ān:

> And in whatever condition you may be, and whatever you may be reciting of the Qur'ān, and whatever work you may be doing, We are witnessing when you are occupied in it. And not so much as an atom's weight on earth or in heaven is hidden from your Lord. And neither is anything smaller than that nor greater, but is recorded in a manifest book (Yūnus 10: 61).

So He himself tells us, 'I am present when you read the Qur'ān': never forget this.

Reciting the Qur'ān is an act of worship. The way to attain highest excellence is worshipping Allah – as the Prophet, blessings and peace be on him, tells us – worship Allah as if you are seeing Him, for even if you cannot see Him with eyes, you can see that He is seeing you (*Muslim*).

Additionally, remember that not only are you in His presence but that He remembers you as long as you are reading the Qur'ān: 'Remember Me and I will remember you' (al-Baqarah 2: 152). The best way to remember Allah, undoubtedly, is to read the Qur'ān.

Hearing from Allah

Third: Say to yourself: I am hearing from Allah.

As a part of your effort to involve your inner self, you should try to think as if you are hearing the Qur'ān from the Sender himself. The Qur'ān is the speech of God. For, just as you cannot see Him while He is always with you, you cannot hear Him while it is He who is speaking. Let the printed words and reciter's voices therefore recede and allow yourself to move nearer to the Speaker. This feeling will be generated and greatly strengthened as your consciousness of 'being in His presence' continues to grow.

Al-Ghazālī, in his *Iḥyā'*, tells about a person who said: I read the Qur'ān but did not find sweetness in it. Then I read it as if I was hearing it from the Prophet, blessings and peace be on him, while he was reciting it to his Companions. Then, I moved a stage further and read the Qur'ān as if I was hearing it from Jibra'īl while he delivered it to the Prophet, blessings and peace be on him. Then God brought me to a further stage – I began to read it as if I was hearing it from the Speaker.

Such feeling will imbue you with a delight and sweetness that will make your inner self fully enveloped by the Qur'ān.

Allah's Direct Address

Fourth: Say to yourself: Allah addresses me directly, through His Messenger, when I read the Qur'ān.

No doubt the Qur'ān was sent down at a specific point in history, and you have received it indirectly through persons, time and space. But the Qur'ān is the word of the Ever-living God, it is eternally valid and it addresses every person. So let all these intermediaries recede for a while and allow yourself to read the Qur'ān as if it is talking directly to you, as an individual and as a member of a collectivity, in your time. The very thought of such direct reception will keep your heart seized by what you are reading.

Every Word for You

Fifth: Say to yourself: Every word in the Qur'ān is meant for me.

If the Qur'ān is eternally valid, and if it *is* addressing you today, then you must take every message as something which is totally and urgently relevant to your life and concerns, whether it be a value or norm, a statement or piece of knowledge, a character or dialogue, a promise or a warning, a command or a prohibition.

Such understanding will make your Qur'ān reading alive, dynamic and meaningful. There may be some problems in translating messages intended for persons who look so different from you into messages relevant to your person and concerns, but with sincere and right effort it should be possible.

Conversation with Allah

Sixth: Say to yourself: I am conversing with Allah when I am reading the Qur'ān.

The Qur'ān contains God's words, addressed to you and meant for you. Though those words are on your lips and inscribed on your heart, they are yet a dialogue between God and man, between Him and you. This dialogue takes many forms. It may be explicit or it may be implicit in the sense that a response is implied from you or Him.

How does this implicit conversation take place? A beautiful example has been given by the Prophet, blessings and peace be on him, in a *Ḥadīth qudsī:*

> I have divided the Prayer [*ṣalat*] between Me and My servant, half is for Me and half for him, and My servant shall have what he asks for. For when the servant says 'All praise belongs to God, the Lord of all the worlds', God says, 'My servant has praised Me'. When the servant says, 'The Most-merciful, the Mercy-giving', God says, 'My servant has extolled Me'. When the servant says 'Master of the Day of Judgement', God says 'My servant has glorified Me' . . . this is My portion. When he says, 'Thee alone we worship and from Thee alone we seek help', He says, 'This is shared by Me and My servant. He will be given what he will ask.' When he says, 'Guide us on the Straight Path ...',

> He says 'This belongs to My servant, and My servant shall have what he has asked for' (*Muslim, Tirmidhī, Aḥmad*).

You will see later how the Prophet, blessings and peace be on him, used to respond with words to the message and content of various verses. Remaining conscious of thus conversing with your Creator and Master will impart an extraordinary quality of intensity and depth to your Qur'ān reading.

Trusting and Expecting Allah's Rewards

Seventh: Say to yourself: Allah will surely give me all the rewards He has promised me through His Messenger for reading the Qur'ān and following it.

Many rewards are promised in the Qur'ān. Assured are the spiritual gifts in life, such as guidance, mercy, knowledge, wisdom, healing, remembrance and light, as well as worldly favours such as honour and dignity, well-being and prosperity, success and victory. Eternal blessings such as forgiveness (*maghfirah*), Paradise (*Jannah*) and God's good pleasure (*riḍwān*), too, are reserved for the followers of the Qur'ān.

The Prophet, blessings and peace be on him, has told about many more rewards. Take any standard Hadith collection like *Bukhārī, Muslim, Mishkāt* or *Riyāḍ al-Ṣāliḥīn,* read the relevant chapters concerning the Qur'ān, and you will find them there. Some of them you will find in this book as well, especially at the end.

For example: 'The best among you is the one who learns and teaches it' (*Bukhārī*). 'Read the Qur'ān, for on the Day of Resurrection it will come interceding for its companions' (*Muslim*). 'No intercessor will be superior in rank to the Qur'ān' (*Sharḥ al-Iḥyā'*). 'On the Day of Resurrection, the companion of the Qur'ān will be told to read the Qur'ān and ascend, as high as the last verse he reads' (*Abū Dā'ūd*). 'For every letter that you read you will get a tenfold reward' (*Tirmidhī*).

Store as many of these promises as you can in your memory and recollect whatever you find relevant, whenever you can. Trust, expect, and seek from Allah their fulfilment in your case.

Observance of such a measure, what the Hadith call *īmānan wa iḥtisāban* (believing and counting), greatly enhances the inner value of your deeds. One Hadith tells that there are forty virtues. If a person performs any of these, hoping for the reward and trusting in the promise, Allah will admit him to Paradise; the highest of these virtues is as little as making a gift of some milk to one's neighbour (*Bukhārī*).

Acts of Heart and Body

There are seven actions of heart and body which will greatly help you in immersing your inner self in the reading of the Qur'ān. Some of these you may already be doing, but you fail to receive their full impact because either you do not do them properly or you are not conscious of what you must achieve through them. Some you are not doing; these are important and you must learn them.

None of these acts requires any more time than you give to your Qur'ān reading now. They only require more attention, greater concentration, and a conscious effort to do things, and to do them properly.

Response of Your Heart

First: Let your heart become alive and respond to whatever the Qur'ān says.

Let everything you read in the Qur'ān react with your heart, and breathe new life into it. Make your heart pass through various corresponding states of adoration and praise, reverence and gratitude, wonder and awe, love and longing, trust and patience, hope and fear, joy and sorrow, reflection and recollection, surrender and obedience. Unless you do so the share you derive from reading the Qur'ān may be no more than the movement of your lips.

For example: When you hear God's name and His attributes, your heart should be filled with awe, gratitude, love and other appropriate feelings. When you read of God's Messengers, your heart should have an urge to follow them, and an aversion for those who opposed them. When you read of the Day of Judgement, your heart should long for Paradise, should tremble at the very thought of being thrown into the Hell-fire, even for a moment. When you read of disobedient persons and nations who went astray and earned God's punishment, you should intensely dislike being as they were. When you read of the righteous whom God loves and rewards, you should be eager to be like them. When you read of the promises of forgiveness and mercy, of plenty and honour in this world, of His pleasure and nearness to Him in the Hereafter, let your heart be filled with a desire to work for them and deserve them. And when you read of those who are indifferent to the Qur'ān, who turn away from it, who do not accept it, who do not live by it – you must fear lest you be one of them, and you must resolve not to be. And when you hear the summons to fulfil your commitment to Him and strive in His way, you should renew your resolve to respond and offer to Him whatever you can.

Sometimes such states of heart will develop spontaneously when some particular word or verse kindles a new spark inside you. Sometimes you will have to make deliberate and determined efforts to induce them. If you do not find an appropriate response spontaneously, pause and repeat what you are reading till you find it. You may find an inner urge to repeat a particular verse many times because your heart demands so, but if you deliberately repeat, pause, and think, you will find your heart quicken.

It is so important to achieve this quality that the Prophet, blessings and peace be on him, once said: 'Read the Qur'ān so long as your hearts are in harmony with it, when they are not in harmony you are not reading it, so get up and stop reading it' (*Bukhārī, Muslim*).

Response of Your Tongue

Second: Let your tongue express in words the appropriate response to what you read in the Qur'ān.

Words, too, should flow spontaneously. For exclamations always flow to reflect your inner feelings as generated by the Qur'ān, as they do for other emotions: cries of joy or anguish, words of thanks, love, fear or anxiety. But, again, even if it is not spontaneous, make an effort.

That is the way the Prophet, blessings and peace be on him, used to read the Qur'ān during the night. Hudhayfah narrates:

> One night I performed my Prayer behind God's Messenger, blessings and peace be on him. He began the reading of the Qur'ān with Surah al-Baqarah ... On every verse mentioning God's mercy he asked God for it, on a verse mentioning His punishment he sought refuge with God. On reading a verse mentioning God's uniqueness and glory, he glorified Him [saying *subḥānallāh*] . . . (*Muslim*).

A similar description is given by 'Abdullāh ibn 'Abbās who once joined the Prophet, blessings and peace be on him, in his night prayers in the quarters of his wife, Maymūnah, who was 'Abdullāh's aunt (*Bukhārī, Muslim*).

Some verses should evoke definite responses, as the Prophet has instructed. For example: Whoever reads the last verse of Surah al-Tīn [Is not God the most just of judges?] should respond with '*Balā wa anā 'alā dhālika mina 'sh-shāhidin* (Yes indeed, I am among the witnesses on this)'; and whoever reads the last verse of al-Qiyāmah [75] shall say 'Balā (Yes, indeed)'; and whoever reads the last verse of al-Mursalāt [77] should say, '*āmannā billāh* (We believe in Allah)' (*Abū Dā'ūd*). The Prophet, blessings and peace be on him, is reported to have said that when he read al-Raḥmān [55] to the *Jinn,* whenever he read the verse – *fa bi ayyi ... tukadhdhibān* – they said, 'No, not anything of Your blessings, Our Lord, we deny; all praise belongs to You' (*Tirmidhī*).

These are but a few instances from what we know of the Prophet's example and teachings. With some reflection, it should not be difficult for you to build up your own responses of praise, glorification, affirmation, denial, and supplication, in the light of these examples: saying *alḥamdulillāh, subḥānallāh, allāhuakbar, lā ilāha illallāh,* or repenting, seeking forgiveness, asking for protection from His displeasure and the Fire, and a place near Him in Paradise.

Tears in Your Eyes

Third: Let the response in your heart overflow through your eyes – tears of joy or of fear – an answer to what you read in the Qur'ān.

If your heart is seized by states which accord with the Qur'ān you are reading, this must happen. Only with an inattentive heart, or a dead and barren heart, will eyes remain dry. The Qur'ān emphasizes this participation of eyes – not always out of fear, but mostly out of joy on finding the truth, on realizing His infinite mercy, on seeing God's promises being fulfilled: 'You see their eyes overflow with tears because of what they have recognized of the truth' (al-Mā'idah 5: 83). And they fall down upon their faces, weeping' (al-Isrā' 17: 109). Often the Prophet, blessings and peace be on him, his Companions, and those like them who had a real encounter with the Qur'ān, would weep when they recited it.

The Prophet, blessings and peace be on him, is reported to have said: 'Surely the Qur'ān has been sent down with sorrow. So when you read it, you make yourself sorrowful' (*Abū Ya'lā, Abū Nu'aym*). According to another Hadith: 'Read the Qur'ān and weep. If you do not weep spontaneously make yourself weep' (*Ibn Mājah*).

Tears will not take long to well up and trickle down your cheeks once you reflect and think about what the Qur'ān is saying, and that it is addressing you. You may make yourself cry, if you think of the heavy responsibilities, the warnings and the good tidings that the Qur'ān brings to you.

Postures of Your Body

Fourth: Adopt an outward posture that reflects your inner reverence, devotion and submission for the words of your Lord.

The Qur'ān tells about such postures in many places: true believers 'fall down upon their faces', they 'prostrate themselves', they 'fall silent and listen when they read the Qur'ān, their skins shiver and soften'. The obligation to prostrate oneself (*sujūd*) on reading certain verses of the Qur'ān is a sure indication of how your bodily postures should reflect what you are reading.

Why are postures of body important? The 'outward' makes a tremendous impact upon the 'inward' of a man. The 'presence' of the body helps keep the 'heart' present. There ought to be a vast difference in your physical attitude while reading the Qur'ān in comparison with an ordinary book. Hence many rules of etiquette and manner have been suggested.

You should, says al-Ghazālī, have *wuḍū'* be soft-spoken and quiet, face the Qiblah, keep your head lowered, not sit in a haughty manner, but sit as you would before your Master. Al-Nawawī, in his *Kitāb al-Adhkār,* adds some more: the mouth should be cleaned thoroughly, the place should be clean, the face should be oriented towards the Qiblah, the body should exhibit humility.

Reading with Tartīl

Fifth: Read the Qur'ān with *tartīl.*

No single word in English can express the full meaning of *tartīl.* In Arabic it means reading without haste, distinctly, calmly, in measured tone, with thoughtful consideration, wherein tongue, heart and limbs are in complete harmony.

This is the desired way of reading the Qur'ān which Allah instructed His Messenger in the very beginning to follow when he was told to spend major parts of his nights standing in prayer and reading the Qur'ān (al-Muzzammil 73: 4). The reason for sending down the Qur'ān slowly and gradually, says Allah, was so that: 'We may strengthen your heart thereby' (al-Furqān 25: 32).

Thus *tartīl is* a significant factor in bringing the heart and the reading of the Qur'ān together, in imparting strength and intensity. *Tartīl,* as compared to hasty babbling, manifests reverence and awe, allows for reflection and understanding, and makes an indelible impression upon the soul.

'Abdullāh ibn 'Abbās is reported to have said: 'I consider reading Surahs al-Baqarah [2] and Āl 'Imrān [3] with *tartīl* better for me than reading the entire Qur'ān hastily. Or, reading Surahs like al-Zalzalah [99] and al-Qāri'ah [101] with *tartīl* and reflection is better than reading al-Baqarah and Āl 'Imrān.'

Tartīl implies not only calmness, distinctness, pause and reflection, and harmony of heart and body, but will also lead to the compulsive repetition of some words or some Ayahs. For, once the heart becomes absorbed and one with a particular Ayah, every time you read it you derive a new taste and pleasure from it. And reading again and again, as we have said, brings the state of heart in harmony with what you are reading.

The Prophet, blessings and peace be on him, is reported to have once repeated, 'In the name of God, the Most-merciful, the Mercy-giving' twenty times (*Iḥyā'*). Once he spent a whole night repeating, 'If Thou punishest them, they are Thy slaves; If Thou forgivest them, Thou art Mighty and Wise' (al-Mā'idah 5: 118) (*Nasā'ī, Ibn Mājah*). Sa'īd ibn Jubayr once kept repeating the verse, 'Separate yourselves today [Day of Judgement], O guilty ones!' [Yā Sīn] – and kept weeping and shedding tears (*Iḥyā'*).

Self Purification

Sixth: Purify yourself as much as you can.

You know that only the 'pure' are entitled to touch the Qur'ān (al-Wāqi'ah 56: 79). This Qur'ānic verse, interpreted liberally, has been taken to mean ritual cleanliness. That you should be ritually clean, with *wuḍū'* (ablution), is established quite well by many Hadith and Consensus (*Ijmā'*). But purity has many more dimensions, apart from the body, dress and space being clean.

You have already seen how important purity of intention and purpose is. Equally important is the purity of the heart and limbs from sins which may incur the anger of the Qur'ān's Sender.

No human being can be completely free from sins; but try to avoid them as much as you can. And if you happen to commit some, try to turn to Allah in repentance and ask for His forgiveness, as soon as you can. Also take care that, while reading the Qur'ān, you are not eating *ḥarām* food, you are not wearing *ḥarām* clothes, you are not living by *ḥarām* earnings (obtained through means prohibited by Allah). The purer you are, the more your heart will remain with you, the more it will open itself to the Qur'ān and understand and derive benefit from it, the more you will be like those who only were entitled to touch 'the noble Qur'ān, in a hidden Book' (al-Wāqi'ah 56: 77-8).

Seeking Allah's Help (Du'ā')

Seventh: Ask Allah for His help, mercy, guidance and protection while you read the Qur'ān.

And seek it with your heart, with your words, with your deeds. In traversing your path through the Qur'ān you must depend utterly and exclusively upon Him. Not only should you be overwhelmed with this sense of dependence, you must express it. You must call upon Him at every step of your journey. You should ask Him to help you in keeping your heart present in understanding the Qur'ān and in following it. Also ask for His forgiveness for your shortcomings and inadequacies.

Beware of any trace of indifference to God and self-sufficiency (*istighnā'*) in approaching God's words. These are great sins. Humility, not pride (*kibr*), dependence (*tawakkul*), not a sense of autonomy, is what you require.

What you ask will be given: this hope, trust and assurance must always remain with you. Without it your *Du'ā'* will not be of much benefit to you. This is one of the most basic teachings of the Qur'ān. Look then at the following verses:

> My Lord, surely in dire need am I of whatever good Thou shalt have sent down upon me (al-Qaṣaṣ 28: 24).
>
> And who despairs of the mercy of his Lord except those who have gone astray (al-Ḥijr 15: 56).

> And your Lord has said: Call upon Me and I will answer you. Surely those who wax too proud to worship Me shall enter Hell-fire, utterly abject (al-Mu'min 40: 60).
>
> I am near. I answer the call of the caller when he calls Me; so let them respond to Me and have faith in Me, so that they go right (al-Baqarah 2: 186).

Let us look at some of the words through which you should seek Allah's help.

Allah's Protection

> I seek refuge with Allah from Satan, the rejected:
>
> *a'ūdhu billāhi mina 'sh-Shayṭāni 'r-rajīm.*

We have already discussed how crucial is the seeking of refuge from Satan. This has indeed been enjoined by the Qur'ān (al-Naḥl 16: 98). Only, do not utter these words like a ritual or a magic formula. Realize that great perils face you in your task, that Satan is your greatest enemy who will do everything possible to deprive you of the rewards of your labour, that Allah, and Allah alone, can protect you against him.

Occasionally, you may like to use longer words for seeking refuge as derived from the Qur'ān (al-Mu'minūn 23: 97), or taught by the Prophet, blessings and peace be on him. Or you may read the last two Surahs: al-Falaq (113) and al-Nās (114).

At times you should also turn to Allah to keep your heart on the right course:

> Our Lord! Let not our hearts swerve from [the truth] after Thou hast guided us [to it]. And bestow upon us Thy mercy. Indeed Thou alone art the Bestower (Āl 'Imrān 3: 8).

While it is obligatory to seek Allah's protection when you begin to read the Qur'ān, the Qur'ānic words suggest that it should be a continuing act. But where you need it most and where you must say it often is when you are trying to understand the Qur'ān.

In Allah's Name

In the name of Allah, the Most-merciful, the Mercy-giving.

Bismi 'llāhi 'r-Raḥmāni 'r-Raḥīm.

The importance and significance of this, too, we have discussed earlier. This verse appears at the head of all but one of the 114 Surahs. Beginning in His name signifies your gratitude to Him for giving you the Qur'ān and your dependence on Him for providing every possible assistance.

Seeking the blessings of the Qur'ān

There are some other specific *Du'ā'* you should try to learn:

> O My Lord! Increase me in my knowledge (Ṭā Hā 20: 114).

Allah instructed the Prophet, blessings and peace be on him, to supplicate in these words while cautioning him to be patient and steadfast in receiving the Qur'ān: And hasten not with the Qur'ān ere its revelation is accomplished unto you.' Seeking support in Allah's name is especially beneficial while one grapples with the meaning of the Qur'ān. Only with patience and Allah's help can the knots be untied and one come to practise the Qur'ān.

Another beautiful *Du'ā'* is:

> O My God! I am Thy slave, son of Thy slave, son of Thy slave-woman.

> I am utterly in Thy possession, my forehead is in Thy hand, Thy every writ is supreme in my affairs, Thy every decision is just and fair.
>
> I ask Thee by every name that Thou hast, that Thou hast called Thyself by, that Thou hast taught any of Thy creation, that Thou hast revealed in Thy Book, or that Thou has kept secret with Thyself.
>
> Make the Qur'ān the spring of my heart, the light of my breast, the dispeller of my sorrows, the eraser of my anxieties and worries (*Aḥmad*).

The following *Du'ā'* is usually said when one completes the reading of the whole of the Qur'ān, but its contents are so comprehensive that frequently calling upon God through these words is sure to provide great blessings:

> O my God! Bestow mercy upon me through the great Qur'ān. Make it for me the leader, the light, the guide, the mercy. God! Remind me by it what I have forgotten, and teach me by it what I know not. Enable me that I read it by night and by day. Make it an argument in my favour. O Lord of the worlds.

Also seek His forgiveness (*Istighfār*) before, during, and after reading the Qur'ān, in whatever words you may choose to do so. Three Qur'ānic expressions you will find in Āl 'Imrān (3: 16), al-Mu'minūn (23: 118), Āl 'Imrān (3: 193).

General Prayers

Apart from these specifically worded *Du'ā'*, you may turn to Allah in your own words and ask Him for various qualities and attitudes you need for benefiting from the Qur'ān: Open my eyes; let me see the truth as Truth and the error as error; bless me with Your light that I may know Your way; support me in my endeavour, strengthen my will; grant me humility at the sight of Your words; grant me joy on receiving Your mercy and guidance; give me guidance in all my anxieties, in all my decisions, in all my affairs; give me resistance against all temptations, strength to perform all tasks, remove my laziness and lethargy; let Your words nourish my thought and action, satisfy my every need; let them bring calm while I am restless, comfort while I am in trouble; help me to study and understand, know and learn about You and Your guidance; grant me perseverance; let me not cease unless I succeed; rid me of my prejudices; grant me humility; grant me strength to accept and obey, and live what I learn; enable me to fulfil the mission that the Qur'ān entrusts to me.

Reading with Comprehension

Last, but not in any way least, by comprehending what you are reading in the Qur'ān you will need to involve your inner person. This may be one of the most important and most effective ways to participate.

While it is obligatory on everyone to understand what the Qur'ān is saying to him before its message can penetrate into the heart, it is not an absolute condition without which one cannot share at all in the blessings of the Qur'ān. There are many who understand every word of it, yet their hearts remain closed to the Qur'ān; there are many who understand not a word yet they achieve intense states of devotion, a relationship with Allah, love and longing, nearness to Him, and obedience. This is because the relationship with the Qur'ān is dependent on many factors - we have listed earlier seven prerequisites - of which understanding is one. There will always be millions who will never learn Arabic nor be able to read a translation nor find time to spend on such pursuits. Yet even they must not despair. So long as they try their best to acquire the means to understand the Qur'ān, so long as they approach it with the necessary conditions, so long as they sincerely attempt to live by the teachings of the Qur'ān as they come to know of them through other sources, so long as they read the Qur'ān even if they do not understand its meaning, they can hope to receive their share of its blessings.

Yet all this can in no way diminish even to the slightest extent the immense importance of understanding what the Qur'ān has got to say to you. Here we are using understanding in the sense of knowing directly what the speech says. The further stages of pondering, reflecting, reaching fuller meaning, making it relevant to our concerns, is something we shall take up later.

Why is merely comprehending the direct meaning necessary? *Firstly,* concentrating on the direct meaning of the Qur'ān will greatly help you in keeping your attention exclusively focused on it, in inducing various states of consciousness and inducing acts of the heart and body necessary for bringing your inner self in a pervasive encounter with the Qur'ān. *Secondly,* only by comprehending will you be able to let the words start the process through which you will acquire and intensify the faith, which will in turn lead you to lives lived by that faith, by the teachings of the Qur'ān.

4

Rules of Reading

Prolonged companionship with the Qur'ān must become one of your most cherished desires and occupations. Read it, therefore, as often and as much as you can. Spend as much time with it as you can find, especially the hours of night. In this manner were the souls of the Prophet, blessings and peace be on him, and his Companions schooled in the way of Allah, to prepare them to shoulder the huge and weighty task that the Qur'ān placed upon them.

There are a few guidelines and rules in this regard that you must bear in mind.

How Often to Read?

Every day you must read some of the Qur'ān. In fact do not consider a day complete unless you have spent some time with the Qur'ān. It is better to read regularly, even if it be only a small portion, than to read long parts, but only occasionally.

Allah likes things which are done regularly, even if little, said the Prophet, blessings and peace be on him (*Bukhārī, Muslim*). He also warned especially that you must attend to the Qur'ān regularly, otherwise you may easily lose your gains. The parable of the companion of the Qur'ān is like a tethered camel; a man holds on to it so long as he attends to it, and it escapes if he lets it loose (*Bukhārī, Muslim*).

How Much to Read?

There can be no fixed answer. It will vary from person to person, and from situation to situation. The guideline must be what Allah, after taking into account all human factors, has said: 'Read whatever you can with ease' (al-Muzzammil 73: 20).

The practice of the Companions and those who followed them varied considerably. Some used to finish the whole Qur'ān in two months, some in one month, some in ten days, some in one week, some even in one day. You should, however, bear in mind the following Hadith as the governing criteria:

> One who reads the Qur'ān in less than three days does not understand it (*Abū Dā'ūd, Tirmidhī*).
>
> Once, when Ibn 'Umar - upon being asked by the Prophet, blessings and peace be on him, to read the Qur'ān in one month - insisted on doing so in less time, he told him: Read it in seven days and do not increase on this (*Bukhārī*).

That the Qur'ān is divided into 7 *ḥizb* (groups) and 30 *juz'* (parts) gives some indication of what is considered desirable.

In this respect al-Nawawī's advice is very sensible: One who can discover deeper meanings by contemplation should read less, similarly one who has to devote time in pursuits like education, affairs of government, or important tasks entrusted by Islam may read less (*Kitāb al-Adhkār*).

The quantity of reading will very much depend on the purpose of reading. If you just want to spend time with the Qur'ān, or get a quick overview, you may read much faster and, therefore, more. If you want to ponder and reflect, you may read much slower and, therefore, less. This is what al-Ghazālī means when he quotes someone as saying 'I complete the reading of the Qur'ān sometimes on every Friday, sometimes every month, sometimes every year. And (in one type of reading) I have been trying to complete it for the last thirty years but have not yet done so' (*Iḥyā'*).

Under our present circumstances, I think, most of us should aim to finish a general reading of the whole Qur'ān at least once every eight months. This should not take more than 5-15 minutes every day, depending on whether you understand the meaning directly or through a translation.

But, at least on a few occasions in your lifetime, you should also attempt to finish one reading in seven days. Or, in one month, especially in the month of Ramadan. Some time should also be devoted to reading slowly, with pondering and reflection, though not necessarily daily.

When to Read?

No time of the day or night is unsuitable for reading the Qur'ān, nor is there any physical posture in which you may not do so. Allah says:

> Remember the name of your Lord at morning and in the evening and part of the night (al-Dahr 76: 25).
>
> Those who remember God when they are standing, and when they are sitting and when they are lying (Āl 'Imrān 3: 191).

Reading the Qur'ān is certainly the best way to remember Him. The Companions and those who followed them, says al-Nawawī, used to read it during all hours of the day and night, whether they stayed in one place or were travelling.

Yet there are some specific times which are more desirable as they are recommended by the Qur'ān and the Prophet, blessings and peace be on him; those moments are more rewarding and fruitful. So too there are certain recommended postures.

The most excellent time to read is at night, and the most desirable posture is to stand in Prayer. In one of the earliest Surahs, al-Muzzammil, as in numerous other places, the Qur'ān tells us so (Āl 'Imrān 3: 113; al-Isrā' 17: 79; al-Zumar 39: 9). It also explains why. Reading the Qur'ān during night-Prayers enables your heart to remain with your reading and strengthens your will in surrendering yourself to Allah's guidance and fulfilling the mission He has entrusted to you.

To do so, however, requires that you should (a) memorize some portions of the Qur'ān, and (b) remain awake for some time during the night. All of you may not therefore be able to do so all the time for various reasons; the Qur'ān recognizes such limitations. It, therefore, permits you to read 'whatever you can do with ease' which means 'whatever portion', at 'whatever time', and in 'whatever position'.

The great need and immense benefits of reading the Qur'ān in Prayer during the night, however, remain. Hence you should assign at least some time, however little, - even a few minutes - with some regular frequency, however long, say weekly or even monthly, for this purpose.

To keep as near as possible to the ideal way, it may be desirable if you read the Qur'ān after or before Fajr and 'Ishā' Prayers, or at dawn, or before going to bed. Reading the Qur'ān at dawn is especially commended in the Qur'ān (al-Isrā' 17: 78).

To read the Qur'ān while sitting on a chair, resting against a pillow, lying in bed or on a couch is not desirable, but is not prohibited. But never do so without excuse, nor make it a habit. However, if one totally misses reading the Qur'ān only because one cannot afford to sit in a proper posture, one loses something more precious.

Reading Correctly

You must read the Qur'ān correctly. At least vowels and letters should be pronounced correctly, even if you are unable to learn the whole art of *tajwīd*. The Arabic language is such that very slight mistakes in pronouncing vowels while reading may drastically alter the meaning, sometimes totally distorting it. On some occasions, you may be saying things which could amount to Kufr.

An hour a day of sustained learning for a month or so should be enough for an educated adult to acquire the minimum essential rudimentary skills in this respect.

No one can be absolved of trying sincerely to learn to read the Qur'ān correctly. But while you are learning, the fact that you cannot do so should not be a reason to forsake your reading. A non-Arab may never master the art of correct reading. Or, you may have no opportunity to learn. The Prophet was aware of such difficulties when he told Jibra'īl, 'I have been sent, Jibra'īl, to a people who are unlettered, among whom are old women and old men, boys and girls, and men who have never read a book' (*Tirmidhī*). You should, therefore, remember his reassuring words in this respect, though do not make them an excuse to shun or slacken your efforts to learn.

> One who is skilled in reading the Qur'ān is with the noble, virtuous angels who bring down the revelation; one who falters while reading it and finds it hard to read correctly, will have a double reward (for reading and for exerting) (*Bukhārī, Muslim*).

Reading Beautifully

Next to reading the Qur'ān correctly, it is desirable to learn the art of *qirā'ah* in order to read it beautifully, in a sweet, pleasant, and melodious style and voice. There are many Hadith which point in this direction:

> Beautify the Qur'ān with your voices (*Abū Dā'ūd*).

> God does not listen to anything as He does to a prophet with a good voice who recites the Qur'ān aloud (*Bukhārī, Muslim*).

> He who does not chant the Qur'ān is not among us (*Bukhārī*).

But remember that the real beauty is the beauty that comes with the fear of God in one's heart:

> His recitation and voice is most beautiful that when you hear him you think he fears God (*Dārimī*).

Listening Attentively

Listen attentively, and fall silent, whenever the Qur'ān is being recited.

This is what the Qur'ān itself commands: 'When the Qur'ān is read, listen attentively, and fall silent, so that you may be blessed with mercy' (al-A'rāf 7: 204). Obviously when God is speaking you must fall silent, but the Arabic word used for 'listening' denotes not merely an act of 'physical hearing' but also a particular state of attention and acceptance.

Consequently, nothing contrary to this instruction should be done; talking or speaking while the Qur'ān is being read; playing *qirā'ah* cassettes and then using it as 'background music' to do other things; talking and whispering, while the Qur'ān is being recited, and opening meetings and functions with the Qur'ān recitation while no one is paying any attention to it.

Some *Fuqahā'* even forbid performing your Prayer while the Qur'ān is being read loudly near you.

This rule also entails that one who is reading the Qur'ān should lower his voice or read silently if his reading aloud places demands on those who are nearby which they will find inconvenient or impossible to meet. This is part of one's duty of being good to one's neighbours; moreover the 'listening' should not be imposed on others unless they so desire.

Asking others, especially those who can read it correctly and beautifully, to read the Qur'ān and, then, to listen to it is also very desirable. The Prophet, blessings and peace be on him, used to ask his Companions to read the Qur'ān to him.

You should bear in mind what the Prophet, blessings and peace be on him, has said in this regard:

> Whoever listens to even one verse of the Qur'ān will be given double the rewards; and for the one who reads, it will become light on the Day of Resurrection (*Aḥmad*).

Completing the Reading (*Khatm*)

The time when you have completed reading the whole of the Qur'ān, no matter how often you may do so, is a time for joy, celebration and prayer. Al-Nawawī mentions certain rules in this regard, drawn from the practices which were usually observed by the Companions and their followers. Although they are not obligatory, they are nevertheless very desirable; observe as many as often as you can.

One: It is better to begin reading on a Friday night and end on a Thursday night. Some preferred to begin at dawn on a Monday. Others picked different times, so that no moment is left without the blessing, and each bears witness on the Day of Judgement.

Two: Read the last portion in Prayer, especially if you finish while you are alone.

Three: Gather other people at the time of finishing, and supplicate together.

When Anas ibn Mālik, the Companion of the Prophet, used to complete the Qur'ān reading, he gathered his family and supplicated (*Abū Dā'ūd*). Ḥakam ibn 'Utaybah is reported to have said: 'Once I was sent for by Mujāhid and 'Ubādah ibn Abī Lubābah who said to me: We have invited you because we intend to finish the Qur'ān, and the supplications at the time of finishing are answered.' In another version they are reported to have said: 'Mercy of God descends at the time of finishing the Qur'ān.'

Four: Fast the day when you intend to complete the Qur'ān reading.

Five: Begin the next reading of the Qur'ān immediately after you have completed the last, i.e. read Surah al-Fātiḥah and a few verses of Surah al-Baqarah after you have finished Surah al-Nās. This will, in one sense, comply with the Hadith narrated by Anas ibn Mālik:

> Among the better of deeds is to [arrive and] settle down and to depart [continue the journey].

When asked what this meant, he replied: 'To end the Qur'ān and to begin it.'

Six: Supplicate and pray at the time of completion of the Qur'ān. It is the time when your supplication is answered and when mercy descends from God. This practice has been very forcefully stressed.

> One who reads the Qur'ān and then supplicates, forty thousand angels say Amin! (*Dārīmī*).

Pray with humility, fearfulness, hope, softness and insistence. Pray for your person, but indeed pray for everything, particularly for the important collective affairs of the Ummah, for its dignity and honour, for the betterment of its rulers, for its safety from hostile forces, for co-operation and unity among Muslims on matters of goodness and *taqwa,* for their standing by the Truth.

Memorizing

Memorize as much of the Qur'ān as you can.

The Qur'ān is unique in demanding to be preserved in memory, the *ḥifẓ*.

The word *ḥifẓ* itself, though now used in the limited sense of memorizing, includes both understanding and practice. In fact there is no English word which can accurately reflect its true and full meaning.

Ḥifẓ is an essential way of making the Qur'ān penetrate you. It is not a mechanical, ritual act; it is an act of high spiritual and devotional importance. Only through *ḥifẓ* can you read the Qur'ān in Prayers and ponder over its meaning while you stand in the presence of the Speaker. But apart from that, it makes the Qur'ān flow on your tongue, reside in your mind, dwell in your heart: it becomes your constant companion. Also as you memorize more you will find it easier to make your inner self participate in its reading and your mind study and understand its meaning.

The Prophet, blessings and peace be on him, has stressed it in various ways:

> Memorize the Qur'ān, for God will not punish the heart which contains the Qur'ān (*Sharḥ al-Sunnah*).
>
> One who has nothing of the Qur'ān inside him is like a desolate/ruined house (*Tirmidhī*).

So allocate part of your time for the Qur'ān for this purpose. Go about it in a systematic way. Set your targets over a period of time. All those parts should form part of your list, which the Prophet, blessings and peace be on him, used to recite during Prayer, or at particular hours of the day and night, or which he instructed his Companions to so recite, or whose excellence he expounded. Some other portions will attract you automatically as you read the Qur'ān regularly, and you should proceed to retain them in your memory.

5

Study and Understanding

Importance and Need

You cannot gather the full and real blessings and treasures of the Qur'ān unless you devote yourself to understanding its meaning, unless you know what your Creator is saying to you.

This is not to deny, as we said earlier, that even those who cannot understand it may partake of its blessings. Obviously an overwhelming majority of Muslims do not know Arabic, and many do not possess any translation in their language. But, if they read the Qur'ān with sincere devotion, reverence and love, they should not fail to share in some of its riches. For, being in the company of the one you love, even if you do not know his language, certainly deepens your relationship with him. Yet immensely greater will be the blessings and stronger will be the relationship if you also understand what he is saying.

On the other hand, merely understanding the meaning may also be of no avail. Many listened to the Qur'ān from the lips of the Prophet, blessings and peace be on him, and understood every word of it; yet they went further astray.

Millions of people for whom Arabic is their language understand the Qur'ān; yet it makes no impact upon their lives. Scores of scholars, Muslims as well as non-Muslims, spend a lifetime studying and reading the Qur'ān, and their scholarship can hardly be faulted; yet they remain impervious to its touch.

Yet, despite this, the urgent need to devote yourself to understanding the Qur'ān remains. The Qur'ān has come as a guide, reminder, admonition and healing. It is not merely a source of reward (*thawāb*), a sacred ritual, a sacrament, a revered relic, or a holy magic. It has come to radically change you and lead you to a new life and existence. Understanding it is no sure guarantee of finding that new life, but without it the task of fulfilling the real purpose of the Qur'ān and inviting mankind to it must remain extremely difficult.

Personal Study

Why have we to devote ourselves to understanding the Qur'ān, on our own, and to thinking, pondering and reflecting upon its meaning? Is it not enough that we read or hear its exposition by the learned? It is most certainly not, even though that too is essential.

You must exert yourself to absorb and discover what the Qur'ān has to say, mainly for one very important, crucial reason. The Qur'ān is not merely a book of knowledge, or a collection of do's and don'ts. It does not merely inform about God and what He wants of you. It also wants to take hold of your person and bring you into a new living and pervasive relationship with Him. Hence, it should increase and strengthen your faith (*Īmān*), your will (*irādah*), your steadfastness (*ṣabr*). It should purify you, form your character, and mould your conduct. It should continually inspire you and elevate you to greater and greater heights.

All this can be accomplished only if you enter into a personal relationship of study, meditation, and understanding with the Qur'ān. Without pondering over its messages, your hearts, your thoughts and your conduct cannot respond to them. Without immersing yourself in thinking and reflecting over them, you cannot absorb them, nor can they impinge upon your life. Just think: Why should reading the Qur'ān with *tartīl* have been enjoined upon you if not for you to ponder and understand? Why should you be required to pause while reading the Qur'an, and how can you make appropriate inward, physical and verbal responses - which the Qur'ān so forcefully emphasizes - if you do not know what you are reading?

Argument Against Studying

But, is there not a danger that a person who is not guided by a learned teacher nor equipped with all the necessary tools of study, and who still embarks on the formidable venture of understanding, on his own, the Book of God, that he may go wrong, even astray? Yes, there is; especially when you do not know clearly your own limitations and goals. But the loss is greater, for yourself and for the Ummah, if you do not try to understand at all. While the risks involved in studying on your own can be averted by taking certain appropriate precautions, and ensuring that you never go beyond your limitations and goals, the loss incurred by forsaking such study cannot be made up.

Does not an attempt to understand the meaning of the Qur'ān on one's own, some argue, violate what the Prophet, blessings and peace be on him, has clearly laid down: 'Whoever interprets the Qur'ān by his own opinion shall take his place in Hell' (*Tirmidhī*)? But this Hadith, obviously, means only such studies as are undertaken to employ the Qur'ān to support and prove one's personal opinions and preconceived notions rather than abandoning oneself, with an open mind, to its guidance. Or to attempt to interpret something for which one does not possess the necessary knowledge. Otherwise, as al-Ghazālī forcefully argues, the Prophet would not have exhorted his Companions to exert themselves to understanding the Qur'ān, nor would they have done so (as they did), nor would they have given meanings which they had not heard from him (as they gave), nor would there have been disagreements between their interpretations (as there are).

Fearful of the consequences, many religious leaders forbid even reading a translation of the Qur'ān without the help of a learned teacher. Or, they lay down conditions for studying alone which only a handful of people, after long, laborious learning, can fulfil. Such counsels, despite their good intentions, in fact end up depriving you of the great riches that the Qur'ān has to offer every seeker. While their fears are genuine, their prohibitions have no logic or basis.

Just think: Can they also prohibit an Arab from understanding the literal meaning of the Qur'ān? Why, then, should a non-Arab not read a translation? Again, can they prevent any person from trying to find the meaning of whatever he reads and seeks to understand? Why, then, prohibit attempts to study the Qur'ān and find its meaning? And finally, what about the first addressees of the Qur'ān, Kafir as well as Muslim? They were illiterate merchants and bedouins, with no scholastic tools in their possession. Yet even some Kafirs were converted by only listening to the Qur'ān, without the help of any learned exegeses, and indeed at the first hearing.

Of course, they had the unique and supreme advantage of 'seeing' the Qur'ānic meaning and message in the lives of the Prophet, blessings and peace be on him, and his Companions, who were living the Qur'ān by going through the crucible of Īmān, Da'wah, and Jihad. We do not, and cannot, have that privilege. Yet even that should not discourage us. There is no reason why the Qur'ān should not open its doors to us once we fulfil the necessary conditions, and most importantly, as emphasized again and again, we, too, live a life of Īmān, Da'wah and Jihad, as the Companions did.

The protection against going astray certainly does not lie in prohibiting every attempt to understand the Qur'ān except by sitting at the feet of a scholar; the cure lies in observing the right guidelines.

This is not to deny the essential need for possessing the necessary knowledge of the Arabic language and of various *'ulūm al-Qur'ān*, of reading *tafsīr*, of learning from qualified and reliable teachers, of being conversant with contemporary human knowledge. They are important, but only to the extent of what you desire to achieve from your study of the Qur'ān. You must possess tools appropriate to your aims, but you cannot dispense with *any* attempt to understand the Qur'ān because you do not possess *all* such tools, or because you are unable to go to a teacher.

Imagine that you are on an 'island'; you do not know Arabic, nor have you any opportunity to learn it; you do not have resources like a good teacher or a good commentary, nor can you acquire one. No doubt you should, under such circumstances, recognize the need of acquiring appropriate capabilities to understand the Qur'ān correctly, make every possible effort to do so. But, even so the Qur'ān remains the guidance for you from Allah.

Fortunately none of us lives on such an 'island'. Such 'islands' come to exist only in our perceptions, mainly due to our lethargy and laziness, inattention and inaction, or our lack of conviction that companionship with the Qur'ān for understanding it is as essential to the nourishment of heart and mind as food is for the body. What is important to remember is that whether or not one really lives on an 'island' with only a copy of the Qur'ān in one's hands, the literal meanings of which one can somehow understand, or whether or not one has mastered all the Qur'ānic disciplines, the need and demand to devote oneself to personally pondering over the Qur'ān remains.

The Qur'ānic Emphasis

The Qur'ān is a guidance for every person, his teacher and mentor. Understanding it is therefore vital; otherwise it will remain no more than a sacrament. The crucial centrality of endeavours, personal endeavours, to open hearts and minds to the messages of the Qur'ān is made abundantly clear by the Qur'ān itself. We are confronted with the utter folly of keeping our hearts locked against our understanding of the Qur'ān:

> What, do they not ponder the Qur'ān? Or, is it that there are locks on their hearts (Muḥammad 47: 24).

Therefore the invitation to bring reason and understanding to the Qur'ān is spread on almost every page of it: Why you hear not? Why you see not? Why you think not? Why you reason not? Why you ponder not? Why you understand not? Why you take not to heart? To whom are these invitations addressed if not to every human being who possesses the faculties of hearing, seeing and thinking?

It is also emphatically declared that the Qur'ān has been sent down to be understood:

> A Book We have sent down, [it is] full of blessings, that men may ponder over its messages, and those who possess understanding may take them to heart (Ṣād 38: 29).

Likewise, the Qur'ān praises as the true 'servants of the Most-merciful' (*'Ibādu 'r-Raḥmān*) those:

> Who, when they are reminded of the revelations of their Lord, fall not thereat deaf and blind (al-Furqān 25: 73).

Conversely, it castigates as worse than animals those who do not use their hearing, sight and hearts to listen, see and understand:

> They have hearts, but they understand not with them; they have eyes, but they see not with them; they have ears but they hear not with them. They are like cattle; nay they are further astray. It is they who are the heedless (al-A'rāf 7: 179).

You cannot gather the real blessings and treasures of the Qur'ān unless you know its meaning, unless you understand what Allah is saying to you, unless you exert yourself personally to find that out.

The Early Practice

The Hadith which discourages reading the Qur'ān in less than three days also makes the need for understanding clear: you will not, then, understand it. One who does not understand the meanings or who does not reflect over them is in no need of this directive. Al-Ghazālī, in his *Iḥyā'*, gives many examples of how the Companions and their followers devoted themselves to this task.

Anas ibn Mālik once said: 'Often one recites the Qur'ān, but the Qur'ān curses him because he does not understand it.' The sign of faith, according to 'Abdullāh ibn 'Umar, is to understand the Qur'ān: 'We have lived long . . . a time has come when I see a man who is given the whole Qur'ān before he has acquired faith; he reads all the pages between al-Fātiḥah and its end, without knowing its commands, its threats, and the places in it where he should pause - he scatters it like the scattering of one fleeing in haste.' 'Ā'ishah once heard a man babbling over the Qur'ān and said: 'He has neither read the Qur'ān nor kept silent.' 'Alī said: 'There is no good in the Qur'ān reading which is not pondered over.' Abū Sulaymān al-Dārānī said: 'I recite a verse and remain with it for four or five nights and do not pass on to another verse unless I have ended my thinking on it.'

Obviously, if the Qur'ān is a book of guidance for every man, the 'man on the island' is as much entitled to receive its guidance as the man immersed in scholarship. If there are no teachers and no books, still you must know it clearly, still devote your time, individually and collectively, to its understanding, to pondering over it, to finding its meaning for your life and finding out what it says to you.

Risks of Personal Study

The risks inherent in such a venture, however, need to be clearly recognized and appropriate measures need to be taken to guard against them. Observing a few guidelines should ensure that you avoid these risks.

Firstly, remember that understanding the Qur'ān is a vast, multi-dimensional process, comprising many types, aspects, degrees and levels. You should know them all. Understanding to nourish the heart will be of a very different order from understanding to derive legal precepts.

Secondly, evaluate yourself and recognize very clearly your limitations and capabilities. For example, evaluate your understanding of the Qur'ānic framework of guidance, your grasp of Arabic, your familiarity with Hadith and Sirah, and your access to sources.

Thirdly, understand your objectives precisely, and set specific goals for your study. Never attempt to do anything beyond what your limitations and capabilities allow.

For example, if you do not know the Arabic language, do not delve into grammatical and lexical issues. Confine yourself to direct, literal meanings. If you have no knowledge of things like *tanzīl* (revelation), *nāsikh-mansūkh* (abrogation), and the works of the earlier jurists, you should not begin to derive your own *fiqh* from the Qur'ān, or criticize and support any particular view.

Fourthly, never take as conclusive nor start propagating any of your findings which are different from or against the general consensus of the Ummah. This is not to bar you from holding your views nor to deny that the opinion of the learned may be wrong, but to controvert or go against them you must possess an equal learning, if not more. Nor does this absolve you from the responsibility to do what you find from the Qur'ān to be morally right and avoid what you find to be morally wrong.

Fifthly, whenever in doubt about your own conclusions, which you may often be in view of your limited knowledge, keep your views 'in suspension' unless you have made a full comparative study or discussed them with a reliable, learned scholar of the Qur'ān.

Categories of Understanding

Broadly speaking, we may divide the study of the Qur'ān into two categories: *tadhakkur* and *tadabbur*, after the Qur'ānic verse: 'That men may ponder over (*li yaddabbarū*) its revelations and . . . may take them to heart (*li yatadhakkara*)' (Ṣād 38: 29).

Tadhakkur

Tadhakkur, used extensively in the Qur'ān, has been translated variously as receiving admonition, deriving advice, remembering, taking heed, and taking to heart. It can therefore be taken to signify the process whereby you try to grasp the general messages and teachings being conveyed by the Qur'ān, to find out what they mean for you and what demands they make upon you, to take them to heart, to bring forth corresponding responses of heart and mind and attitudes, to have the will to act in accordance with whatever you find, and, finally, to determine what message you have to deliver to your fellow human beings.

Tadhakkur is a category of understanding which, in its essential nature, should not require any sophisticated tools of scholarship. You may not know the meaning of every word, you may not be competent enough to explore the full meaning of all the important and key words, and you may not understand every verse, but the general, overall message, especially the message for you - how to live - should come out clearly and radiantly.

After all, the people who understood the Qur'ān most and benefited from it the greatest were its first hearers - they were city merchants, farmers, shepherds, camel riders and nomads. They did not have at their elbows lexicons, *tafsīr* books, treatises on style, diction, cadence, rhetoric nor did they possess all the knowledge of philosophy, history, geography, archaeology, anthropology, or of the social and physical sciences. Yet they were the most successful in understanding the Qur'ān. For, they took the message of the Qur'ān to their heart and began to live it. Hence this category of understanding *ought* to be and *is* available to every person who fulfils the necessary condition for it in this respect. The degree and intensity of what he receives will depend on his effort and capacity. Of course, tools of scholarship may add new dimensions, lend added weight, give new insights, to this process; but they are not a must.

It is in the sense of *tadhakkur* that the Qur'ān categorically states that it is easy to understand, it is available to *every* sincere inquirer if he only comprehends what he is reading and ponders over it. It is to this *tadhakkur* that the Qur'ān invites everyone who can hear, see and think, to be guided by it. It is in this sense that it says:

> Indeed we have made this Qur'ān easy for understanding and remembering (*dhikr*). Is there any, then, that will take it to heart (*muddakir*)? (al-Qamar 54: 17).
>
> Indeed we have made it [the Qur'ān] easy [to understand] by your tongue [O Prophet] so that men might take it to heart (*yatadhakkurūn*) (al-Dukhān 44: 58).
>
> Indeed We have made propounded unto men all kinds of parables in this Qur'ān, so that they might understand (*yatadhakkarūn*) (al-Zumar 39: 27).
>
> In this there is indeed a reminder (*dhikr*) for everyone who has a heart, or will give ear while he is a witness [present with his mind] (Qāf 50: 37).

Tadhakkur is not some lower category of understanding; it is the basic essential purpose of the Qur'ān. You will have to strive all your life in order to gain the light and guidance and healing through *tadhakkur* – and through this process you, personally, must continue to gather an unlimited number of gems.

Tadabbur

Tadabbur is the other category of understanding. It signifies that you try to find the full meaning of every word, Ayah, and Surah, that you explore the fuller meaning behind those words, metaphors and parables, that you discover the textual cohesion and underlying unity, that you determine the central ideas, delve into lexical intricacies, *tanzīl*, and historical background, and that you undertake a comparative study of different *tafsīr*. Then, that you discover all the implications for the relationship between man and his God, his fellow human beings, his own self, and the world around him; that you derive laws and morals for individuals and society, rules for state and economy, principles for history and philosophy, and implications for the current level of human knowledge.

Such a study would require a greater and deeper knowledge of various *'ulūm al-Qur'ān* (the Qur'ānic disciplines), depending on your goals and aims.

Tadabbur and *tadhakkur* are not entirely separate nor mutually exclusive categories of understanding, they overlap.

Your Aims

What should your aims be? Obviously aims will vary from person to person and, even for a person, from time to time. *Tadhakkur*, in my view, is obligatory for every Muslim who is or can become capable of understanding the Qur'ān.

Hence, as an average-educated Muslim, who is trying to fulfil his commitment to Allah in the light of his capabilities and limitations, *tadhakkur* should be your first aim, and the most important one. You will stay with it forever; you will never reach a stage where you may dispense with it.

In *tadhakkur*, remember, you essentially set out to nourish your heart and mind, to increase your faith, to discover the message that the Qur'ān is giving to you, to take it to heart, to remember it. Through all your labours you should be able to hear God's voice: what He wants you to be and to do.

Levels and Forms of Understanding

Your understanding of the Qur'ān may have various levels and take different forms.

Firstly, that you comprehend its simple, literal meaning, as when you read a book in a language you know, or as an Arabic-knowing person would understand the Qur'ān.

Such comprehension must be the bare minimum requirement, the key to all other stages, but it is not enough.

Secondly, that you find out how the learned have understood it, either by hearing their expositions or reading their exegeses and other sources.

Thirdly, that you study and ponder, on your own, to discover and absorb its meaning, to attain *tadhakkur* and, if you have the capability and need, then *tadabbur* as well.

Fourthly, that you discover its meaning by obeying its messages and by fulfilling the duties and mission that it entrusts to you.

Basic Requirements

There are certain basic requirements which you should fulfil in order to make your endeavours fruitful.

Arabic

One: Try to learn at least as much Arabic as will enable you to understand the meaning of the Qur'ān without the help of a translation. This is the first step, the most essential prerequisite.

It may seem an arduous task, but I have known semi-illiterate persons accomplish this within a few months, once they took to it seriously and devotedly. With the help of a teacher, or even a suitable book, you should not require more than 120 hours of study to learn enough Arabic to comprehend what the Qur'ān is saying.

But do not postpone your endeavours to study the Qur'ān till such time as you learn Arabic. Take a good translation, or the best available, and start your pursuit. This is still better than reading the Qur'ān without any comprehension.

Reading the Whole Qur'ān

Two: Read, first, the whole Qur'ān, from beginning to end, comprehending the direct, literal meaning. If you do not know Arabic then use a translation.

Indeed you should make a special project of completing the first reading of the Qur'ān in *one month.* This should not take more than two hours a day. After that you can settle down to a slower pace as may be convenient for you. But you must continue with such overview reading throughout your life, at whatever pace suits you, as you have already come to know under the rules of reading.

An initial reading of the whole Qur'ān is very important before you embark on a deeper study. This will give you the general overall message of the Qur'ān, some idea of its style and diction, argument and rhetoric, and a view of its teachings and injunctions. Reading it regularly, you become familiar with the Qur'ān; you feel its cohesive unity and begin to look at it as a unified whole; you are in less danger of interpreting something outside the general framework of the Qur'ān. Those who go to the Qur'ān through concordances, instead of their own familiarity with its contents and contexts, are quite liable to fall into error in their interpretation.

Keeping company with the text of the Qur'ān regularly is an essential key to understanding it as a whole; it will be of immense help, too, in understanding even single words and Ayahs. By prolonged and sustained company you will find that many a time you will come across a text which will suddenly seem to speak to you and answer your questions.

Indeed, at any one time, you may be making your way through the Qur'ān in a variety of ways to achieve different aims. You may be engrossed in a rapid reading, to finish it in a definite period of time. Or, you may be spending hours to locate the meaning of one single word or one single verse. You may be reading one passage, again and again, sometimes rapidly, sometimes slowly, to ponder over its meaning. Or, you may be flipping through the pages - once you have become familiar with the whole ground - to find guidance on a particular issue or theme. You may be thinking on your own, which may take less time; or you may be making a comparative study of short and long *tafsīr* works, which may make you stay with a small portion for a long time.

Reading Tafsīr Works

Three: Once you have completed one reading of the whole Qur'ān with comprehension, and you are keeping up with regular reading at the slower pace that you find feasible, take a short and reliable *tafsīr* or notes, and read it through. Quite a few good short commentaries are available in Arabic, Urdu and other major Muslim languages, though presently English and European languages are very deficient in this respect. However, whatever is available can be profitably used, if read cautiously.

Reading a short commentary or notes will give you a more detailed view of the Qur'ān than what you have acquired on your own. It will introduce you to important areas like language, style, argument, historical background, detailed meanings, something which you cannot discover by your own thinking and reflection. It may also correct some of your errors.

Try to confine yourself to short commentaries whenever you need help in your personal detailed study of the Qur'ān, and do not delve, at least initially, into long, elaborate exegetical works.

Often their long discourses become a barrier to your direct, living relationship with the word of God. Read partial commentaries, if no full commentary is available. Also, while reading literature on Islam, make a special note of whatever you find centred on the Qur'ān in the discourses and conclusions you read. Even though widely scattered, you may find very useful aids to understanding in such works.

Remember that nourishment for Īmān and the essential message on how to live is available to you without detailed exegeses. Only to remove some doubt, to investigate a fine point, to untie a knot will you require the help of a *tafsir.*

Study of Selected Portions

Four: Ideally you should start a study of the Qur'ān from the very beginning and carry it through to the end. One day, *inshā'llāh* some of you will undertake such a venture, but for most of us that day may be too far away, or may never come. You should, however, start your own study as soon as you can.

For this purpose, then, take up short selections, passages, Surahs or even an Ayah, and study them in greater detail. Sometimes, your involvement in self-improvement and Da'wah will oblige you to study particular portions. Sometimes, your regular reading may throw up certain passages you would like to take up. But you may also follow a systematically formulated thematic syllabus. The important thing is to start and know how to study, not what to start with. Some suggested passages are listed at the back of this book.

To start studying selected passages will benefit you in many ways. *Firstly,* you will begin making progress on one of the most important parts of your journey through the Qur'ān by establishing the very essential relationship of *tadhakkur* with it, rather than waiting indefinitely. *Secondly,* you will acquire important clues, keys and methodologies which will help you to understand even those parts of the Qur'ān which you may not be in a position to study immediately in detail; for it repeats its messages in manifold forms (al-Zumar 39: 23). *Thirdly,* you will develop a fuller perception of the total Qur'ānic framework, so essential for keeping your understanding on the right course. *Fourthly,* you will become better equipped to communicate the message of the Qur'ān to fellow human beings.

A detailed study of selected passages, however, can never be a substitute for general reading, the benefits of which are of a different nature and importance. Do not, therefore, give up your regular reading of the Qur'ān or longer sections, as emphasized earlier. Attending to detail and ignoring the whole may distort your vision and understanding.

Reading Again and Again

Five: Whatever part you have chosen to study you will have to read again and again. Take this as a maxim you should always follow. Stay with it as long as you can, live with it, dwell in it and let it dwell in your heart and mind. Such prolonged companionship is an essential key to understanding meaning. As the Qur'ānic words become engraved on your heart, as they are frequently on your lips, you will find it easier and more rewarding to contemplate and meditate upon them. Then, not only during the time you have set aside for study, but even during your everyday life the Qur'ān will disclose its meaning to you as the words and Ayahs keep coming back to your mind.

Inquiring Mind

Six: Develop an inquiring mind, a searching soul, a heart hungry for meaning. The Qur'ān, as you already know, does not require a blind faith, nor does it ask you to read it with ears closed, eyes shut, and minds locked. Invitation to think is one of its most persistent and pervasive themes.

To question, remember, is the key to understanding and knowledge. So, always raise as many questions as you need to. For example: What does this word or verse literally mean? What other meanings can be construed? What is the historical background, occasion of revelation, if known? What is the context of each word, phrase, and sentence? How does each link with what precedes and succeeds it? What internal order and thematic unity can be discerned? What is said? Why is it said? What are the general and specific implications? What are the major themes? What is the central theme? What is the message for me, us, now? Make a note of your questions and try to find their answers as you continue your study and reading.

Do not be frightened of raising questions. You may not find their answers immediately or ever on your own, or even with proper help. That does not matter. Whatever you can find an answer for will be a gain. You stand to lose nothing only if you observe certain rules. *Firstly,* do not ask questions the answers to which may be beyond human competence, which belong to *mutāshābihāt* (Āl 'Imrān 3:7): such as, what is the *'Arsh* like? *Secondly,* do not indulge in hair-splitting nor ask questions which have no relevance to the implications of the passage for your life. *Thirdly,* do not try to give answers that are not based on appropriate and necessary knowledge or sound reasoning. *Fourthly,* there will be questions which you cannot find answers for, which you cannot understand, despite your best efforts. Leave them for a while and pass on to other things in the Qur'ān. A time will come when you will find a teacher or book to help you. Or, you may find the answers even on your own.

There is enough evidence within the Qur'ān about how its first believers used to ask questions. Equally significant and instructive are numerous instances where the Prophet, blessings and peace be on him, and his Companions used to encourage inquiry, questioning and thinking.

Aids for Study

Seven: There are certain aids which you will require to help you in your study. Try to acquire as many of them as you can.

(1) Have a copy of the Qur'ān with a translation in your language. This is the minimum that you will require. This you should use for both general reading and study. The same can be used for memorization, if it is handy.

But, take care that throughout life you stick with the same copy for memorization, otherwise revision will be difficult.

Remember, too, that no translation can be perfect or accurate. Each translation contains an element of interpretation by the translator. There is not, and cannot be, an 'authorized' translation of the Qur'ān.

(2) The same copy may contain a short commentary, or you may have to acquire one separately. But you must have one. A translation and a reliable commentary should be enough for your initial, main objectives.

(3) You may find it useful, though it is not necessary, to have more than one translation and commentary to investigate various meanings of words and text as understood by different scholars.

(4) For more advanced study, you should have at least one more detailed *tafsīr.* You may not find one in English; but, then, try to acquire whatever part-*tafsīr* works are available.

(5) Have a good Arabic dictionary, preferably a Qur'ānic dictionary, to enable you to look deeper into the meanings of words.

(6) Have a concordance.

A few such suggested aids for study are listed at the back of this book.

How to Study

Below a step-by-step procedure for studying in detail any selected passage is suggested. There are, however, no fixed rules about it. Indeed you may find it more useful to develop a procedure of your own which suits your capabilities and limitations better. What is important is that you proceed in a systematic way, and try to observe the following sequence.

First, you study the passage entirely on your own. Next, consult your study aids or go to a qualified teacher to learn whatever you can about its meanings. Finally, combine your learning from both phases to arrive at such fuller understanding as you can.

Stage I: Acquaint yourself and define your problems.

Step 1: Recollect very quickly what you can remember of the basic prerequisite and inner participation. Realize that Allah is with you and pray to Him to help you understand what you are going to read.

Step 2: Read the passage, comprehending its meaning, at least thrice, or as many times as is necessary to enable you to recollect its broad contents without looking at it. Then you will have absorbed it and will be able to think on it whenever you desire.

The rule is: let the words and meanings soak in before you begin to look for interpretation.

Step 3: Note down, without reading the text, all *major themes* that you can discern. Then check these with the text, and revise.

Step 4: Note down the central theme, if you can discern one.

Step 5: Divide the passage into such shorter portions which you think convey one single message or group of messages.

Step 6: Underline all words and phrases that you think are central to understanding the meaning.

Step 7: Ask questions, as we have explained above, and note them down.

Stage II: Think over what you have read: try, on your own, to answer your questions, and understand the meaning and message within the framework of guidelines outlined in the next section.

Step 8: Find what the important words mean.

Step 9: Determine the meanings of each phrase or statement.

Step 10: Think how they are interlinked, why one follows or precedes another, what unity and cohesion there is.

Step 11: Find and understand the meaning within the immediate context of the passage, the larger context of the Surah, the overall context of the Qur'ān.

Step 12: Determine what are its various messages and teachings.

Step 13: Ask: What does it say to me and for our time?

Step 14: Think how you, the Ummah and mankind are required to respond.

Stage III: Try to find meaning from whatever study aids or teachers you may have, and go through Stage II (steps 8-14), with their help. Revise, correct, modify; enlarge, affirm, or reject, your own understanding.

Stage IV: Write down or preserve in your mind and heart the understanding so arrived at.

Make note of whatever questions remain. Do not take any understanding to be complete and final: you will continue to find more meaning and realize the need for revision as you continue your study.

How to Understand Meanings

The principles and guidelines that should be followed in understanding the Qur'ān are many and it would require a long treatise to discuss all of them in sufficient detail. Here we can only outline, that too only briefly, some important ones that you must always bear in mind while trying to understand meanings.

General Principles

Understand as a Living Reality

One: Understand every word of the Qur'ān as if it was being revealed today. Take it as relevant and living a Book for our modern times as it was when first sent down fourteen centuries ago. For, as it is eternally valid and immutable, in a sense it can give no different message now. Do not, therefore, take any verse of the Qur'ān as merely a thing of the past. Only then will you understand it as the 'living' word of the Ever-living God who sustains all creation every moment (*al-Ḥayy al-Qayyūm*)

As you have seen, it is essential for your heart to participate in your reading. Your mind and intellect, too, should approach the Qur'ān with this reality guiding them all the time. Its implications are enormous. This will enable you to translate everything in the Qur'ān so that you can understand your world in its light.

In this light, then, try to relate and apply it to your own life. The prevalent concerns, issues, experiences and levels of knowledge and technology of your time - should all find an answer in the Qur'ān.

Understand as a Message for You

Two: Take, more importantly, every message in the Qur'ān as being addressed to your person, to your community. Once you have made some progress, you should try to understand what lesson each Qur'ānic text is giving for your personal situation. You have seen earlier how it should be done to increase your inner participation. Now, you must realize how it will open your mind to understanding the Qur'ān.

One man came to learn the Qur'ān from the Prophet, blessings and peace be on him, who taught him Surah al-Zalzalah (99). When he reached the words, And so, he who has done an atom's weight of good, shall see it; and he who has done an atom's weight of evil, shall see it', the man said, 'This is sufficient for me', and left. The Prophet, blessings and peace be on him, observed: 'This man has returned back as a *faqīh* (who has acquired understanding)' (*Abū Dā'ūd*).

Indeed, I believe there is not a single passage in the Qur'ān which does not have a personal message for you, only you have to have the insight to look for it. Every attribute of God asks you to build a corresponding relationship with Him, every description of the Life beyond death asks you to prepare for it, or aspire for its reward, or seek protection from its evils, every dialogue involves you in it and every character presents a model you should either emulate or avoid following. Every legal injunction, even if it is apparently inapplicable in your present situation, has some message for you. Very general statements always have a specific meaning for you;

very specific statements, events and situations can always lead to general propositions to apply to your lives.

Understand as a Part of the Whole

Three: The whole Qur'ān is a unity within itself. It is a single revelation. The message itself, though conveyed in manifold and diverse forms, is one message. It has one world-view, one total framework of guidance. All parts are therefore fully consistent with one another. This is one sign of its Divine authorship.

> What! Do they not ponder the Qur'ān? Had it been from any but God, surely they would have found in it much inconsistency (al-Nisā' 4: 82).

This single message and framework you should try to fully grasp. Everything, then, you must understand as a part of this message, of the whole Qur'ān as a single Book – whether it be a single word, an Ayah, a paragraph or a Surah. Never tear anything away from the total Qur'ānic framework, otherwise you may arrive at distorted meanings. Check whatever meaning you arrive at for consistency by placing it in the overall context.

While studying selected passages, you will have to analyse it, dissect it and understand each sentence, even each word, separately. But do not forget to put them back together to give the single picture, and then put that single picture within the overall message of the Qur'ān. Without this, your selective study may lead you in opposite directions. Without this, you may fall into the error of using selected verses to support your viewpoint instead of being guided to the Qur'ānic view.

Also you should bring the whole of the Qur'ān to your study as you try to find meaning which will apply to your time and problems. Otherwise you may commit the grave mistake of making the

Qur'ān conform to contemporary thought rather than critically evaluating it in the light of the Qur'ān.

It is not advisable, in view of the above, to approach a study of the Qur'ān through a concordance, as said earlier. Indeed, unless you have read the Qur'ān many times over and have fully understood its total framework, do not study any subject by collecting verses through a concordance. Use it only when you are looking for references you require on the basis of your study.

Understand as a Coherent Unified Text

Four: The Qur'ān possesses coherence and order of the highest degree, despite the apparent randomness you observe. Each part is related to the other, Ayah with Ayah, Surah with Surah. Behind the apparent fluctuations of themes there is a unifying thread. That is why the Prophet, blessings and peace be on him, used to instruct the scribers where to place a particular revelation.

This internal cohesive order you should try to find, even though you may not discern it at your first attempt, or indeed it may take a long time to reveal itself to you. Only when understood within the context of this order, will each part yield its fuller meaning to you.

Understand with the Whole of Your Being

Five: Understand by applying the whole of your being to the study of the Qur'ān. Both heart and mind, feeling and intellect are fused together in your person. The Qur'ān is not a parcel to be intellectually unwrapped, nor merely a beatitude to be ecstatically experienced. Do not approach the Qur'ān as a split person; leave neither intellect nor feeling behind you when you study it; let both come together.

Understand What the Qur'ān Tells You

Six: Understand what the Qur'ān tells you, not what you tell the Qur'ān. Never go to the Qur'ān to seek support for your opinion, to confirm your view, to prove your case. You must approach it with an open mind, ready and prepared to listen to God's voice and surrender to it.

Stay Within the Consensus

Seven: You are not the first to study and understand the Qur'ān. Before you there was a continuous chain of people who took up this task, and who have compiled a rich heritage. You cannot ignore them. You should not therefore approach the Qur'ān as if no one had ever approached it before, nor make your way around past interpretations. No meaning arrived at can be valid which contradicts what the Prophet, blessings and peace be on him, has expounded or practised, or on which a consensus exists in the Ummah. Conclusions which are new or radically different from the rich heritage handed down from generation to generation, should be based on sound scholarship.

Understand by the Unique Qur'ānic Criteria Alone

Eight: The Qur'ān is not like any other book; it is unique in every respect. It has its own language and diction, style and rhetoric, logic and argumentation, and, above all, a unique approach and purpose. To measure and understand it by extra-Qur'ānic, human, standards and criteria will be of no avail.

Its unique purpose is to guide man, every man, to his Creator, to radically change him by bringing him into a totally new relationship with his God. Everything is directed towards this goal, is informed and shaped by this objective. This has some important implications.

Firstly, though the ocean of its meaning has no depth and no shore, the meanings that are enough to guide an average seeker after truth on how to live his life, are plain and intelligible, in some degree, to him, whenever he approaches it in true spirit and in the right way.

Secondly, its language is such that a common man can understand it. It uses words taken from common parlance, used in everyday conversations. It does not coin new, unintelligible terms, nor does it use the technical, academic language of philosophy, science, logic, or any other discipline. It does impart, however, radically new meanings to old, everyday words.

Thirdly, it is neither a book of history nor of science, neither of philosophy nor of logic, though it uses all of them, but only to guide man. Hence do not try to make the Qur'ān confirm any contemporary human knowledge, nor is that knowledge essential to understand it. Though one can always derive help from it to increase comprehension.

Fourthly, the Qur'ānic method of argumentation is based on man's everyday experience of nature, history, and his self. It is unique in confronting its hearer in his own world that he recognizes, on his own premises that he accepts. That is how it captures his heart and mind, and changes them.

Understand the Qur'ān by the Qur'ān

Nine: The best *tafsīr* of the Qur'ān is the Qur'ān itself. It, seemingly, repeats many of its words and discourses. But in fact it is not pointlessly repetitive; repetition of a particular word or discourse usually sheds new light on its meaning, or brings into focus a new aspect. That meaning you should try to understand.

So, to understand the meaning of any word, or Ayah, or passage, look into the Qur'ān itself. For example, you may better understand key words like *rabb, ilāh, dīn, 'ibādah, kufr, īmān, dhikr,* by studying them in the various contexts that the Qur'ān has used them.

Understand with the Hadith and Sirah

Ten: One of the Prophet's main duties, blessings and peace be on him, was to explain the Qur'ān. This he did through his words and example. Hence the entire corpus of Hadith and Sirah forms a rich source for understanding the Qur'ān. Not only the Hadith which particularly contain *tafsīr* material, but all Hadith are helpful. For example, the Hadith on themes like Īmān, Jihad, *tawbah,* will help you greatly in understanding the Qur'ānic verses where you come across similar themes.

Language

Eleven: Language is your first key to the Qur'ān. Together with the life of the Prophet, blessings and peace be on him, it is crucial to its understanding. Through language the Qur'ān makes itself clear, alive and understood. Some characteristics of the Arabic as used in the Qur'ān you should remain aware of.

Firstly, the Qur'ānic style is that of the spoken word, not written. An address may leave certain things unsaid, which the direct hearers are supposed to find no difficulty in providing. This enhances its effectiveness and power; for the hearers are continually interacting with the speaker, his word, and their environment. Too many details make an address wooden. There are sudden changes of tenses as well. They, too, add to the lively impact of the text. You will have to remain alert to these changes and determine who is addressing whom. There are sudden breaks too; you will have to identify them.

Secondly, not only that, the Arabic language in its expression is highly concise and elliptical. It often does not use connecting words and phrases. Hence there are ambiguities, omissions, suppressions, substitutions and other characteristics like these, which you will have to remain careful about. These you may learn only from *tafsīr* works or teachers.

Thirdly, direct literal meanings of words and texts, in isolation, are not enough to understand them or the text fully. You will have to acquire some understanding and feel of the overall world-view, literary style and idiom of the Qur'ān. Acquaintance with the Arabic literature as it was at the time of revelation will be of immense help, though as a beginner it may be initially beyond your reach.

Methodological Guidelines

Within the framework of the above general principles, some methodological guidelines should be useful for you.

Studying Words

One: First, try to determine the meanings of those words which you find crucial to the understanding of the text. Your initial guides will be the translation and the short commentary that you have. Consult the dictionary as well, but do not consider dictionary renderings adequate. Your best and final guide is the immediate context of the word, as well as the whole Qur'ān and its world-view.

Textual Context

Two: Once you understand the words and the direct, literal meaning, place the passage in its textual context and try to understand what it means. Read the preceding and succeeding texts, also the whole Surah if necessary.

Historical Background

Three: Collect as much historical information as you can find and as is necessary and relevant. But ensure its authenicity.

In this connection, you will come across Hadith giving 'reasons of revelation' (*asbāb al-nuzūl*). They may give valuable information, but keep two things in mind: firstly, such narratives may not always tell exactly about the historical occasion when the revelation came, but rather the situation to which it was considered relevant and applicable. Secondly, the textual evidence about the occasion of revelation is more important; it should not be set aside while accepting historical information. Thirdly, historical information should not act as a constraint on your understanding in applying the text to your situation.

'Original' Meaning

Four: After comprehending the direct, literal meaning, try to understand, as best you can, how the text may have been understood by its first hearers. Finding the literal meaning may be an easier task; finding the 'original' meaning, fourteen centuries later in a different civilizational context, will be a difficult and complex task. This is not the place to discuss these difficulties, only to caution you.

Translating to Your Situation

Five: Your next task should be to read and understand the text in your own context. This too is as formidable a task as determining the original meaning, especially if you do not wish to fall into the trap of reading your context into the Qur'ān. Again, it is not possible here to discuss the complex problems of interpretation in this regard, nor do I dismiss them lightly. But this is a task you cannot ignore or avoid. If you remain mindful of one elementary principle and observe it – come to the Qur'ān with an open mind and never make it say what you think is right – you may avoid such traps. Also, concentrate on the essential message for your life, rather than on complex legal and moral issues.

It is possible, sometimes even necessary, to employ contemporary terminology to elucidate and bring into focus the real intent and import of the Qur'ān for our situation, but only so long as the direct, clear and original meaning is maintained, and the original terminology is not lost.

Far-fetched and Irrelevant Meanings

Six: Do not concern yourself with discovering such far-fetched, allegorical, inner meanings which no ordinary person can ever understand. Nor look for meanings which have no relevance to your life or to the lives of the Qur'ān's first believers.

Level of Knowledge and Intelligence

Seven: Understand meanings at the level of intelligence and knowledge that you possess. However, do not lose sight of the level of knowledge that its first addressees had, so that you do not go astray and begin to read your own knowledge into the Qur'ān.

Current Human Knowledge

Eight: There is no escaping the fact that each person will employ his own knowledge to understand the Qur'ān. Indeed, you need to have this knowledge in order to critically evaluate it by Qur'ānic criteria, to seek guidance from the Qur'ān on the issues it raises, and to understand the Qur'ān in current idiom. Again, by all means bring your knowledge to help you understand the Qur'ān, but never bring the Qur'ān to confirm contemporary knowledge. Do not make the Qur'ān foretell all the scientific discoveries of our day. Especially, remain cautious about scientific theories, which are like shifting sand. It would be as wrong to read into the Qur'ān Einstein or Copernicus, Nietzsche or Bergson, as it is to read Ptolemy, Aristotle and Plato.

What You Cannot Understand

Nine: There will be many words and sentences, that you will not be able to understand after every effort. It may be because you do not possess enough knowledge, or because it is too difficult. In such cases make a note of your difficulties and then pass on to other studies. Do not spend time grappling with things which may, at some stage, lie beyond your competence.

Life of the Prophet

To understand and absorb the Qur'ān, you must come as close as you can to the Prophet, blessings and peace be on him, who received it first from Allah. His life is the best 'exegesis' of the Qur'ān, the surest guide to its meaning and message. It is the 'living Qur'ān'. If you want to see the Qur'ān rather than merely read it, see the Prophet, blessings and peace be on him. For, as Sayyidah 'Ā'ishah said, 'his conduct was nothing but the Qur'ān'. You will find his Sirah much more helpful in understanding the Qur'ān than great exegetic works like *Ibn Jarīr, Ibn Kathīr, Kashshāf* and *Rāzī*.

To move closer to the Prophet, you should, firstly, read his sayings, the Hadith, and his life, the Sirah, as much as you can. You will also find the Qur'ān to contain the best account of his Sirah, even if there are no biographical details. And, secondly, try to follow his Sunnah. By doing so you will really understand him and, therefore, the Qur'ān. Also you will love Allah and Allah will love you (Āl 'Imrān 3: 31).

6

Collective Study

Importance and Need

Your journey through the Qur'ān requires that you seek and join a community of quest and study. No doubt you will read the Qur'ān individually, but your benefits will multiply if you also join in fellowship with other believers and seekers after the Qur'ān. In companionship, the states of the heart may be intensified, and many minds joined together may understand meanings better and more correctly. And, only by joining with others can you live fully the lives inspired by the Qur'ān and discharge the mission that reading it enjoins upon you. By acting and fulfilling that mission you will deserve to be admitted to the fullest possible blessings of the Qur'ān.

Significantly, the Qur'ānic address is almost always collective. And the Prophet, blessings and peace be on him, from the moment he received the revelation of the Qur'ān, set out to create a community with the Qur'ān at the centre of its life, and spent every moment of his life in this effort. The instruction to 'read' was followed, in time, by the command to 'arise and warn'. The instruction to continue to 'read what has been revealed to you in the Book of your Lord' is immediately followed, contextually, with the instruction to 'bind yourself with those who call upon their Lord at morning and evening, desiring His countenance, and let not your eyes turn away from them' (al-Kahf 18: 27-8). These Qur'ānic teachings clearly and forcefully establish the link between its reading and the need for a strong, closely-knit community rooted in that reading.

Again, no Prayer can be complete without reading the Qur'ān, nor, if it is obligatory and there is no genuine excuse, without fellowship with others (*Jamā'ah*). What is the purpose of reading the Qur'ān in Prayer if not to hear it, understand it and ponder over it? Thus five times a day this purpose should be accomplished in collective endeavour.

The duty to communicate the message of the Qur'ān to the whole of mankind also entails that the Qur'ān should be read and explained corporately. The word *tilāwah,* when used with the Arabic preposition *'alā,* means to communicate, to propagate, to spread, to teach. To do the *tilāwah* in this way is one of the basic functions of the Prophethood, and, therefore, of his Ummah (al-Baqarah 2: 129, 151). In Surah al-Jumu'ah (62), failing to understand and live by Divine guidance is emphasized in the context of failing to stay with the Friday Prayer for which every worldly activity must be given up.

The Qur'ān also hints at the reading of the Qur'ān in families and homes in the following verse: And remember that which is recited in your houses of the revelations of God and the Wisdom' (al-Aḥzāb 33: 34).

Those who gather together to read and study the Qur'ān are blessed because upon them descend the angels with God's abundant mercy, as the Prophet, blessings and peace be on him, said:

> Whenever people gather in one of the houses of Allah for reading the Qur'ān and teaching it to one another, peace descends upon them, mercy covers them, angels spread their wings over them, and Allah mentions them to those around Him (*Muslim*).

So you should not be content with reading and studying the Qur'ān alone, but should set out to find other seekers and invite them that you may do so together.

Forms of Collective Study

Collective study may take two forms.

One: Where a small group gathers to study and deliberate upon the Qur'ān so that each participant takes an active part in the process, though some among them may be more knowledgeable than others and one will lead the study. This we shall call '*Ḥalaqah*', (after the above Hadith), or Study Circle.

Two: Where a group, small or large, gathers to study the Qur'ān by actively listening to the exposition given by a knowledgeable person. The participants only raise questions. This we shall call '*Dars*', lesson or lecture.

You should know how a Study Circle should be conducted and how to prepare and deliver a Dars. Here we can discuss only very broad guidelines. Again, it is important to remember that there can be no standard, fixed procedures. Each person or group will have to develop his or their own method, and each situation will have to be treated on its own. The guidelines given below are only suggestions which you should adapt to your requirements and capabilities.

Four Basic Rules

Four rules are basic to the success of any collective study.

One: You must always make all the preparations necessary to fulfil your responsibility. Do not take your task lightly, do not postpone your preparation till the eleventh hour, do not consider a quick glance enough, never say anything about the Qur'ān without having given it full consideration. It is always better to make note of what you have studied and what you want to say.

Two: Whether you are a novice or you already possess some knowledge, whether you have to give Dars or participate in discussion in a circle, undertake a study on your own of the selected part, broadly in line with the procedure described earlier.

Three: Always keep your *niyyah* right, that is, understand and live the Qur'ān in order to seek Allah's pleasure.

Four: Do not study together merely for pleasure, intellectual curiosity, or argument and discussion. Your studying the Qur'ān together must result in your obeying the Qur'ān together and fulfilling the mission it entrusts to you.

Study Circle

The following guidelines should help in making the group study effective.

Participants

One: The number of participants should be 3-10; with no great divergence in the levels of their knowledge and intelligence. Anything less will make it a dialogue, anything more may hinder the active participation of everyone.

Two: The stress should always remain on the message, context and what guidance and lessons are to be drawn. Never get entangled in fine points which have no relevance to real life.

Three: All members should be fully aware of their aims, limitations and procedures.

Four: All members should have the necessary commitment to their task and realize that time, attention and hard work will be required. It is especially important that regular preparation and attendance are observed.

Five: All members should know how to find their way through the Qur'ān. A study of this book may be of some use.

Six: The group members should not sit as strangers, but as brothers in faith in the Qur'ān, committed to understanding and obeying it.

How to Conduct a Study Circle

One: One member should, first, make a presentation of the results of his study.

Two: The rest should then join in, further elaborating, correcting, modifying, raising questions, or providing answers.

Three: If all the members are required to study, then you may either designate beforehand who will do the presentation; this will result in better standards of presentation. Or, call upon anyone present to do the presentation; this will keep everyone alert and working hard.

Four: It will always be useful if at least one member of the circle is more knowledgeable and has access to sources. He would, then, during the discussion, overcome any deficiencies and shortcomings in the original presentation. He may also set and steer the tone and direction of discussion.

Five: If one member who is learned in the Qur'ān participates, he should not intervene from the beginning. Rather he should let the participants say what they want to say, and only then, gently correct them if they are wrong, or add to their knowledge. His method should be suggestive and interrogative rather than discursive.

Six: Towards the end, one member, preferably the leader or teacher, should always sum up the broad message of the passage, its main themes, and its call to action.

Dars

The following guidelines may help to make a Dars effective.

Preparation

One: Have a fair idea about the audience: such as, their level of knowledge and intelligence, their state of Īmān, their concerns and worries, and their needs and requirements.

Two: Select the passage in keeping with the state of your audience, rather than what you find yourself eager to expound.

Three: The nature and level of your style, language, exposition should correspond to the nature of your audience.

Four: Pray to Allah to help you in bringing the true message of the Qur'ān to your listeners.

Five: Study the passage and write down your notes: what do you want to say? In what order? How? How do you begin? How do you end?

Six: Give due regard to the time at your disposal. Never exceed your time. You may have a lot of good points and be very eager to pour them all out. But, remember, your listeners have a very limited capacity to retain. They may admire your learning and erudition, but may not learn very much from it.

Long passages can always be dealt with in a short duration and short passages can be dwelt upon for a long duration. It all depends on what you think you have to communicate from the passage under study.

Seven: Give full attention as to what clear message or messages, out of all that you may say, you would like to leave with the listeners for them to retain, reflect and act upon.

This must conform with the central idea of the passage, not with your own desires.

How to Deliver

One: You must have only two aims:

Firstly, to seek Allah's pleasure by doing your duty in making others hear His words.

Secondly, to communicate the message of the Qur'ān clearly and effectively.

Two: Remember that it lies in the hands of Allah to make your communication effective in reaching your listeners' hearts and minds.

But this does not absolve you from your responsibility for doing your best to prepare as best you can, to deliver as effectively as you can, to bring the message of the Qur'ān in a manner as makes it living and dynamic for them, to make it relevant to their concerns, to make it bear upon their situation.

Your delivery may not be of high oratorial or rhetorical standards, it may be very ordinary – but it is your *niyyah* and effort that count.

Three: You may first read the whole text and give its translation, and then take up the exposition, with or without reading each verse and its translation again. Or, you may give a brief introduction and start by taking up one verse after another, or a group of verses. What procedure you adopt will depend on the time at your disposal and the situation.

Remember that it is not essential to read the whole passage and its translation in the beginning, especially if time is short. You may spend the time better in preparing the listeners for what they are going to hear.

Four: As far as the individual verses or groups of verses are concerned, you may use a mixture of various approaches. If the verse is clear and short, you may first read it and then elaborate. You may turn to the theme before and after your exposition.

What you must ensure is that your listeners get a sense of cohesive unity - each statement should be seen to flow from the preceding one and lead to the next.

Five: At the end, you must sum up the contents, and emphasize the message. You may also, if you have time, even read the whole text again, or only the translation. Reading the text or translation towards the end serves to bring your listeners in direct contact with the Qur'ān after they have understood what it means in light of your exposition.

Six: Always be on guard that it is the Qur'ān which must speak, and not you. The Qur'ān has been effective, without any exposition, for those who knew the language and the Messenger. It still is. You may hinder the Qur'ān from speaking not only by inserting your own views too much, but also by your very lengthy and elaborate explanations. By the time you finish your long discourse, your listeners may very well forget what the Qur'ānic text said.

So, *firstly*, keep your explanations as short as possible; and, *secondly*, if they have to be long as may be necessary in some instances, you should refer back to the text as often as possible. You should create no distance between the listeners and the text of the Qur'ān, not only in meaning, but also in hearing.

Seven: Model your own exposition on the pattern and style of the Qur'ān. This may be the most effective means of ensuring the success of the occasion.

Initially you may find it difficult, but gradually - as you move nearer to the Qur'ān, read it often, memorize it - it will become part of your own style.

You must remember certain characteristics of the Qur'ānic style. *Firstly*, that it appeals to both reason and feeling, intellect and soul as one whole. *Secondly*, that it is short, precise, direct, personal, and evocative. *Thirdly*, that it confronts its listeners with choices and decisions and inspires them to heed and act. *Fourthly,* that its language is as powerful as the message, which penetrates deep inside you. *Fifthly,* that its argument is always what its listeners are able to understand, that it is always drawn from their everyday experience, that it always finds an echo inside them. Above all, that it is not abstract, logical, speculative.

Eight: Do not make overly abstract statements, nor conceptualize and systematize at the cost of the Qur'ān's dynamic impact. Concepts and systematic presentation are vital to the presentation of the Qur'ān's message, but so long as they are made in simple and ordinary language and within the grasp of the audience. Calls to action; summons to commit, must be essential ingredients of your Dars. Whether it is nature or history, injunction or statement, dialogue or address - each should result in some call to respond, to come forward, to decide and to act.

Nine: Do not use the Qur'ān as a pretext to propound your views, instead make yourself an exponent of the word of God.

Ten: Let the Qur'ān make its way to your listeners hearts, let it reside there, let it stir impulses of recognition, love, gratitude and awe: this should be the thrust of your Dars.

Eleven: Always remain attentive to the response of your audience. You can always cut an argument short or give up what you may consider valuable to impart, if you feel that it does not interest them or arouse them. You can always introduce new points, styles, and emphasis, depending on what you feel are the demands of the situation.

7

Living the Qur'ān

Obeying the Qur'ān

Reading the Qur'ān will be of little benefit to you, it may even bring misery and harm, unless you, from the first moment, begin to change and reconstruct your life in total surrender to God who has given you the Qur'ān. Without the will and striving to act, neither the states of heart and enraptures of the soul, nor the ecstasies of mood, nor intellectual enrichment will be of any use to you. If the Qur'ān does not have any impact upon your actions and if you do not obey what it enjoins and avoid what it prohibits, then you are not getting nearer to it.

On every page of the Qur'ān is an invitation to surrender and submit, to act and change. At every step the reader is confronted – to decide and commit himself. Those who do not submit to it are declared to be *Kāfir, ẓālim* (wrongdoer) and *fāsiq* (iniquitous) (al-Mā'idah 5: 44-7). Those who are given the Book of God but do not understand it nor act upon it are described as 'asses which carry loads', but neither know nor benefit from what they carry (al-Jumu'ah 62: 5). They are those against whom the Prophet, blessings and peace be on him, will plead on the Day of Judgement:

> O my Lord! Behold, [some of] my people have taken this Qur'ān as a thing to be shunned (al-Furqān 25: 30).

To shun the Qur'ān, to leave it, and to put it aside, means not to read it, not to understand it, not to live by it, to consider it a 'thing of the past', which has ceased to be relevant.

The Prophet, blessings and peace be on him, is no less emphatic in stressing the necessity of obeying the Qur'ān:

> Many of the hypocrites in my Ummah will be from among the readers of the Qur'ān (*Aḥmad*).
>
> He is not a true believer in the Qur'ān who treats as *ḥalāl* (permissible) what it has made *ḥarām* (prohibited) (*Tirmidhī*).
>
> Read the Qur'ān so that it enables you to desist [from what it prohibits]. If it does not enable you to desist you have not really read it (*Ṭabarānī*).

For the Companions of the Prophet, to learn the Qur'ān amounted to reading it, pondering over it, and acting by it. It is narrated that:

> Those who were engaged in reading the Qur'ān told that people like 'Uthmān ibn 'Affān and 'Abdullāh ibn Mas'ud, once they had learnt ten verses from the Prophet, blessings and peace be on him, did not go any further unless they had really 'learnt' whatever these verses contained by way of knowledge and practice [understood them and acted upon them]. They used to say that they learnt the Qur'ān and knowledge together. That is how they sometimes spent years in learning only one Surah (*al-Itqān fī 'Ulūm al-Qur'ān,* Suyūṭī.

Al-Ḥasan al-Baṣrī said: 'You have taken the night to be a camel that you ride on to pass through various stages of the Qur'ān. Those before you considered it as messages from their Lord; they pondered over them at night and lived by them by day' (*Iḥyā'*).

Reading the Qur'ān should induce faith inside your heart; that faith should shape your lives. It is not a gradual, piecemeal process, by which you first spend years reading the Qur'ān, then understanding it and strengthening your faith, you only then act upon it. The whole is one unified process, all things take place simultaneously. As you hear or recite the words, they kindle faith inside you; as you have faith inside you, your life begins to change.

What you must remember is that to live by the Qur'ān requires a major decision on your part: you have to completely alter the course of your life, irrespective of what may be the dominant thought-patterns around you, of what your society may be dictating, or what others may be doing. This decision requires major sacrifices. But unless you, as believers in the Qur'ān being the word of God, are prepared to take the plunge, not much good will come out of the time you spend with the Qur'ān.

From the very first moment, at the first step, it is made abundantly clear that the Qur'ān is a guidance for those who are prepared to act to save themselves from the harm that comes from living against God's will, from earning His displeasure, and who fear the consequences - they are the *al-muttaqīn* (al-Baqarah 2: 1-5). The Qur'ān does not recognize any polarity between knowledge and action, between faith (*Īmān*) and righteous deeds (*al-'amal al-ṣāliḥ*)

Fulfilling the Qur'ān's Mission

An essential and important part of living by the Qur'ān is to convey its message to people around you. Indeed the moment the Prophet, blessings and peace be on him, received the first revelation he realized the immense task of bringing it to his people. And the second revelation came with the summons: 'Stand up and warn' (al-Muddaththir 74: 2). Then at various places it was made clear to the Prophet, blessings and peace be on him, that to communicate the Qur'ān, to make it heard, to explain it was to be his primary duty, his life mission (al-Anʿām 6: 19; al-Furqān 25: 1; al-Anʿām 6: 105; al-Mā'idah 5: 67; Maryam 19: 97; al-Aʿrāf 7: 157).

Now we, as his followers, as people possessing the Book of God, are charged and entrusted with the same mission. To have the Qur'ān obliges us to convey it; to hear the Qur'ān is to make it heard. We must make it clear and known to mankind and not let it remain concealed:

> And when God took pledge from those who had been given the Book: 'You shall make it known to mankind, and not conceal it.' But they cast it behind their backs, and bartered it away for a small price – how evil was their bargain (Āl ʿImrān 3: 187).

If there is a lamp in your heart and hand, it must spread its light. If there is fire inside you, it must radiate its warmth and glow.

Those who do not do so, for want of transient worldly gains, are in fact filling their bellies with fire:

> Those who conceal of what the Book of God has sent down on them, and barter it away for a little price – they shall eat naught but the Fire in their bellies, God shall not speak to them on the Day of Resurrection, neither purify them (al-Baqarah 2: 174).

And they deserve the curse of Allah:

> Those who conceal the clear messages and the guidance that We have sent down, after We have made them clear for mankind in the Book – they shall be cursed by God and the cursers (al-Baqarah 2: 159).

Unless they discharge their duties:

> Save such as repent, and put themselves right, and make [the Book] known – towards them I shall turn ... (al-Baqarah 2: 160).

But, if they die in this condition, they will be cursed by all and everyone:

> But those who remain in [the state of] disbelief, and die disbelieving - upon them shall be the curse of God, and the angels, and of all men ... (al-Baqarah 2: 161).

God will not even look at them:

> Those who barter away their covenant with God, and their pledges, for a little price, they shall not partake in the blessings of the life to come; and God shall not speak to them, neither look at them on the Day of Resurrection, neither will He purify them ... (Āl 'Imrān 3: 77).

Look at yourself! Look at Muslims today! Why, despite the fact that the Qur'ān is read by millions day and night, does it make no difference to our situation? Either we read it and do not understand it; or, if we understand it, we do not accept it nor act upon it; or, if we act upon it, we accept part of it and reject part of it; or, while we are engrossed in reading it and acting by only part of it, we are guilty of committing the worst crime and concealing it and not bringing its light to the world.

> And some among them are illiterate common people, who have no knowledge of the Book, [believing] only wishful fancies, and they depend on nothing but conjecture. Woe, also, unto those who write [the meanings of] the Book with their own hands, then say, 'This is from God', that they may acquire thereby a little price ... (al-Baqarah 2: 78-9).
>
> What! Do you believe in part of the Book and disbelieve in part? What, then, shall be the reward of those of you who do that but ignominy in the life of this-world and, on the Day of Resurrection to be returned unto the most grievous suffering (al-Baqarah 2: 85).

Let there not be the slightest doubt in our minds that unless we commit ourselves to the most important responsibility of being witnesses unto the Qur'ān, which devolves upon us by virtue of us having it and reading it, we shall never discharge what we owe to the Qur'ān. The ignominy, dishonour, humiliation, backwardness that has become our lot is only because of the way we treat the Qur'ān and the mission it entrusts to us.

> By this Book God makes some peoples to rise and others to decline (*Muslim*).
>
> Had they established the *Tawrāh,* and the *Injīl,* and what has been sent down to them from their Lord, they would have eaten from above them and from beneath their feet (al-Mā'idah 5: 66).

Nor shall we succeed in discovering and understanding the full and real meaning of the Qur'ān, whatever Qur'ānic scholarship we may attain, unless we obey the Qur'ān. The Prophet, blessings and peace be on him, said to his Companions:

> There will be such people among you that, when you will compare your Prayers with theirs, your Fasts with theirs, your good deeds with theirs, you will consider yours very inferior. They will read the Qur'ān, yet it will not sink deeper than their throats (*Bukhārī*).

To surrender and obey is not only to fulfil the real mission of the Qur'ān, it is one of the surest keys to its understanding. You discover a meaning by obeying that you never discover by mere thinking. You, then, begin to 'see' the Qur'ān. Writes Syed Mawdudi in memorable words one can hardly forget:

> ... but all that you may do to understand the Qur'ān is not enough. If you want to identify with the spirit of the Qur'ān, you must practically involve yourself with the struggle to

fulfil its mission. For the Qur'ān is not a book of abstract theories and cold ideas, which one can grasp while seated in a cosy armchair. Nor is it merely a religious book like other religious books, whose meanings can be grasped in seminaries and oratories.

On the contrary, it is a Book which contains a message, an invitation, which generates a movement. The moment it began to be sent down, it impelled a quiet and pious man to abandon his life of solitude and confront the world that was living in rebellion against God. It inspired him to raise his voice against falsehood, and pitted him in a grim struggle against the lords of disbelief, evil and iniquity. One after the other, from every home, it drew every pure and noble soul, and gathered them under the banner of truth. In every part of the country, it made all the mischievous and the corrupt to rise and wage war against the bearers of the truth.

This is the Book which launched a glorious movement, with the voice of a single individual, and continued to provide guidance to it for twenty-three years, till the establishment of the Kingdom of God on earth. At every stage during this long and heart-rending struggle between truth and falsehood, this Book showed its followers the ways to eradicate the old order and usher in the new.

Is it, then, possible to reach the heart of the Qur'ān merely by reading its words, without ever stepping upon the battlefield of faith and disbelief, of Islam and Ignorance, without passing through any stage of that struggle? No, you can understand the Qur'ān only when you take it up, begin to act upon it, and call mankind to God, and when every step you take is in obedience to its guidance.

Then, and only then, you will go through all the events and experiences which occurred during the course of its revelation. You will then pass through *makka,* and *ḥabash,* and *ṭā'if;* you will face *badr, uḥud, ḥunayn* and *tabūk*. You will encounter *abū jahl* and *abū lahab;* you will meet with hypocrites and *jews;* you will come face to face with those who instantly responded to this call as well as those who were drawn into Islam seeking some gain. You will come across all of these human models; you will deal with all of them.

This is a path different from the so-called 'mystic path', which I name the 'Qur'ānic path'. Such is this 'Qur'ānic path' that, as you pass through its various stations and stages, certain Surahs and Ayahs will disclose their full message to you, and tell you that they were revealed precisely for this stage and station that you are passing through. You may miss some linguistic and grammatical subtleties, you may miss certain finer points in the rhetoric and semantics of the Qur'ān, yet it is impossible that the Qur'ān will fail to reveal its full and true spirit to you.

In the same way, no person can ever understand the legal injunctions, the moral teachings, and the political and economic directives of the Qur'ān, unless and until he puts them into practice. Neither the individual who lives independently of the Qur'ān nor the nation which runs its institutions in violation of its guidance can discover the spirit of the Qur'ān (*Tafhīmul Qur'ān,* Vol. I, Lahore 1979, pp. 33-4).

Appendix 1

What the Prophet Particularly Read or Emphasized

There are certain Surahs or Ayahs of the Qur'ān which, it is reported, the Prophet, blessings and peace be on him, used to recite more often in particular Prayers or on specific occasions, or which he especially extolled by describing their excellent merits and special rewards. You should know them.

The Hadith given below are not meant to prove the superiority of one part of the Qur'ān over another. Nor should you ignore the rest of the Qur'ān and occupy yourself in reading and memorizing these at the expense of the rest. These selections are useful only because one cannot memorize and read everything every day and because one usually needs to habituate oneself to the reading of a definite portion regularly. What could be better than to follow the Prophet, blessings and peace be on him, and hope for the rewards he has promised.

It is important to remember that the Prophet, blessings and peace be on him, used to recite the whole of the Qur'ān at least once in the month of Ramadan. He also recited long portions in the night-prayers, as much as Surah al-Baqarah and Āl 'Imrān in one *rak'ah*.

What the Prophet Recited in Various Prayers

In the Fajr Prayer

He used to recite *Qāf* (50) and similar Surahs, reports Jābir ibn Samurah (*Muslim*).

He recited *al-Wāqi'ah* (56) (*Tirmidhī*).

I heard him reciting *al-Takwīr* (81), reports 'Amr ibn Hurayth (*Muslim*).

He recited, while in Makka, *al-Mu'minūn* (23), until verse 45 or 50, reports 'Abdullāh ibn al-Sā'ib (*Muslim*).

He recited *al-Kāfirūn* (109) and *al-Ikhlāṣ* (112), reports Abū Hurayrah (*Muslim*).

He recited *al-Falaq* (113) and *al-Nās* (114), reports 'Uqbah ibn 'Āmir (*Aḥmad, Abū Dā'ūd*).

He recited verses from *al-Baqarah* (2: 136) and *Āl 'Imrān* (3: 64), reports 'Abdullāh ibn 'Abbās (*Muslim*).

Abū Bakr al-Ṣiddīq is reported to have recited *al-Baqarah* (*Muwaṭṭā'*).

'Uthmān ibn 'Affān very often used to recite *Yūsuf* (12) (*Muwaṭṭā'*).

'Umar ibn al-Khaṭṭāb recited *Yūsuf* (12) and *al-Ḥajj* (22) (*Muwaṭṭā'*).

'Umar wrote to Abū Mūsā to recite *ṭiwāl mufaṣṣal* [from Surah *Muḥammad* (47) to *al-Burūj* (85) (*Tirmidhī*).

The Prophet recited *al-Kāfirūn* (109) and *al-Ikhlāṣ* (112) in the two *rak'ahs* before Fajr, reports Abū Hurayrah (*Ibn Mājah*).

In the Fajr Prayer on Fridays

He recited *al-Sajdah* (32) in the first *rak'ah,* and *al-Dahr* (76) in the second, reports Abū Hurayrah (*Bukhārī, Muslim*).

In the Ẓuhr and 'Aṣr Prayers

He used to recite *al-Layl* (92) and, according to another version, *al-A'lā* (87), and similarly in 'Aṣr, reports Jābir ibn Samurah (*Muslim*).

He used to recite *al-Burūj* (85) and *al-Ṭāriq* (86) and similar Surahs, reports Jābir ibn Samurah (*Tirmidhī*).

'Umar wrote to Abū Mūsā to recite *awsāṭ mufaṣṣal* [from Surah *al-Burūj* (85) to *al-Bayyinah* (98)1 (*Tirmidhī*).

In the Maghrib Prayer

I heard him reciting *al-Mursalāt* (77), reports Umm al-Faḍl (*Bukhārī, Muslim*).

I heard him reciting *al-Ṭūr* (52), reports Jubayr ibn Muṭ'im (*Bukhārī, Muslim*).

He used to recite *al-Kāfirūn* (109) and *al-Ikhlāṣ* (112), reports 'Abdullāh ibn 'Umar (*Ibn Mājah*), especially on Friday nights, reports Jābir ibn Samurah (*Sharḥ al-Sunnah*).

He recited *al-Dukhān* (44), reports 'Abdullāh ibn 'Utbah (*Nasā'ī*).

He recited *al-A'rāf* (7), reports 'Ā'ishah (*Nasā'ī*).

He recited *al-Kāfirūn* (109) and *al-Ikhlāṣ* (112) in the two *rak'ahs* after Maghrib, reports 'Abdullāh ibn Mas'ūd (*Tirmidhī*).

'Umar wrote to Abū Mūsā to recite *qiṣār mufaṣṣal* [from Surah *al-Bayyinah* (98) to *al-Nās* (114)] (*Tirmidhī*).

In the 'Ishā' Prayer

He instructed Mu'ādh ibn Jabal to recite *al-Shams* (91), *al-Ḍuḥa* (93), *al-Layl* (92), and *al-A'lā* (87); and not longer Surahs like *al-Baqarah,* reports Jābir (*Bukhārī, Muslim*).

I heard him reciting *al-Tīn* (95), reports al-Barā' (*Bukhārī, Muslim*).

In the Jumu'ah and 'Īd Prayers

I heard him reciting *al-Jumu'ah* (62) in the first *rak'ah,* and *al-Munāfiqūn* (63) in the second, in the Jumu'ah, reports Abū Hurayrah (*Muslim*).

He used to recite *al-A'lā* (87) and *al-Ghāshiyah* (88) in the Jumu'ah and both the 'Īd Prayers, and if the Jumu'ah and 'Īd fell on the same day he recited the same Surahs in both, reports al-Nu'mān ibn Bashīr (*Muslim*).

He used to recite *Qāf* (50) and *al-Qamar* (54) in *al-Aḍḥa* and *al-Fiṭr,* reports Wāqid al-Laythī (*Muslim*).

What the Prophet Recited at Various Times

At Tahajjud

After getting up from sleep, 'he looked towards the sky and recited *inna fī khalqi 's-samāwāt* . . . till the end of the Surah' [Āl 'Imrān 3: 190-200], reports 'Abdullāh ibn 'Abbās (*Bukhārī*).

In the Morning and Evening

Al-Ikhlāṣ (112), *al-Falaq* (113), *al-Nās* (114) three times: Recite them in the morning and in the evening and 'they will suffice you for every purpose', reports 'Abdullāh ibn Khubayb (*Tirmidhī, Abū Dā'ūd*).

Āyatu 'l-Kursī and Hā mīm ... al-maṣīr (*al-Mu'min* 40: 2-4): Anyone who recites them in the morning 'will be protected because of them till the evening and anyone who recites them in the evening will be protected because of them till the morning', reports Abū Hurayrah (*Tirmidhī*).

Last three Ayahs of *al-Ḥashr* (59: 22-4): if one recites these in the morning, 'seventy thousand angels ask forgiveness for him until the evening, and if he recites it in the evening they do so until the morning', reports Mi'qil ibn Yasār (*Tirmidhī*).

Three Ayahs of *al-Rūm* (30: 17-19): 'If one recites it in the morning, he is rewarded for whatever good he neglects during the day, and if he recites it in the evening, he is rewarded for whatever good he neglects during the night', reports 'Abdullāh ibn 'Abbās (*Abū Dā'ūd*).

Before Going to Bed or During the Night

Recite *Āyatu'l-Kursī* when going to bed (2: 255): He confirmed that 'a protector from Allah will then remain over you, and Satan will not come near you, until the morning', reports Abū Hurayrah in a long Hadith about his encounter with Satan (*Bukhārī*).

When he went to his bed, 'he joined his hands and breathed into them, reciting into them ... [*al-Ikhlāṣ*], ...[*al-Falaq*], ... [*al-Nās*]. Then he would wipe as much of his body as he could with his hands, beginning with his head, his face and the front of his body, doing that three times', reports 'Ā'ishah (*Bukhārī, Muslim*).

Recite the last two verses of *al-Baqarah:* 'Who reads them during the night, they would suffice him', reports 'Abdullāh ibn Mas'ūd (*Bukhārī, Muslim*).

Last part of *Āl 'Imrān* (3: 190-200): it will be rewarded like the night vigil.

Al-Dukhān: (44) 'Seventy thousand angels will ask forgiveness for him in the morning', reports Abū Hurayrah (*Tirmidhī*).

Recite *Musabbiḥāt* [*al-Isrā'* (17), *al-Ḥadīd* (57), *al-Ḥashr* (59), *al-Ṣaff* (61), *al-Jumu'ah* (62), *al-Taghābun* (64), *al-A'lā* (87)]: 'He used to read them before going to sleep and say "they have a verse better than one thousand verses"', reports al-'Irbāḍ ibn Sāriyah (*Abū Dā'ūd, Tirmidhī*).

Al-Sajdah (32) and *al-Mulk* (67): 'He did not sleep unless he had recited them', reports Jābir (*Aḥmad, Tirmidhī*).

What the Prophet Said About the Excellent Merits of Various Parts

The Prophet, blessings and peace be on him, is reported to have said:

Surah al-Fātiḥah (1)

'Shall I not teach you the greatest Surah in the Qur'ān', said he, and then taught *al-Fātiḥah* and described it as 'the great Qur'ān [recital] I have been given', reports Abū Sa'īd al-Mu'allā (*Bukhārī*).

'Rejoice in the two lights brought to you which have not been brought to any prophet before you': *al-Fātiḥah* and the last verses of Surah *al-Baqarah* (2: 285-6), said an angel to the Prophet, blessings and peace be on him, reports 'Abdullāh ibn 'Abbās (*Muslim*).

'By Him in whose hands is my soul, nothing like it has been sent down in the *Tawrāh,* nor in the *Injīl,* nor in the *Zabūr,* nor in the Qur'ān', reports Abū Hurayrah (*Tirmidhī*).

'It is a healing for every sickness', reports 'Abd al-Malik ibn 'Umayr (*Dārīmī*).

Surah al-Falaq and Surah al-Nās (*113 and 114*)

'The like of these have never been seen', reports 'Uqbah ibn 'Āmir (*Muslim*).

'No seeker of refuge can seek refuge with anything like these two', reports 'Uqbah ibn 'Āmir (*Abū Dā'ūd*).

Surah al-Ikhlāṣ (112)

'Is any of you incapable of reciting a third of the Qur'ān in a night?' asked he, and then proceeded to instruct: recite *al-Ikhlāṣ*, 'for [by the One in whose hands is my life], it is equivalent to [reading] a third of the Qur'ān', reports Abū Sa'īd al-Khudrī (*Bukhārī, Muslim*).

'Tell him that Allah loves him', said he about a man who recited it in every Prayer because it described the Most-merciful, reports 'Ā'ishah (*Bukhārī, Muslim*).

'Your love for it will admit you into Paradise', he said to a man who loved *al-Ikhlāṣ*, reports Anas (*Tirmidhī, Bukhārī*).

Surah al-Kāfirūn (109)

'It is equivalent to a quarter of the Qur'ān', report 'Abdullāh ibn 'Abbās and Anas ibn Mālik (*Tirmidhī*).

Surah al-Naṣr (110)

'It is equivalent to a fourth of the Qur'ān', reports Anas (*Tirmidhī*).

Surah al-Takāthur (102)

'Cannot one of you recite one thousand verses in one day' asked he, and then said 'cannot one of you recite *al-Takāthur*', reports 'Abdullāh ibn 'Umar (*Bayhaqī*).'

Surah al-Zalzalah (99)

'It is equivalent to half the Qur'ān', report 'Abdullāh ibn 'Abbās and Anas ibn Mālik (*Tirmidhī*).

Āyatu'l-Kursī (*al-Baqarah 2: 255*)

'Do you know which Ayah in God's Book is greatest', he asked, and then showed his approval when told that this was *Āyatu 'l-Kursī*, reports Ubayy ibn Ka'b (*Muslim*).

Āmana 'r-rasūl ... (*al-Baqarah 2: 285-6*)

'No prophet before has been brought a light like it', reports 'Abdullāh ibn 'Abbās (*Muslim*).

'In whichever home these are recited for three nights, Satan does not come near it', reports al-Nu'mān ibn Bashīr (*Tirmidhī*).

'It is from the treasures of God's mercy from under His Throne that He has given to this Ummah. There is no good in this-world and that-world which it does not include', reports Ayfa' ibn 'Abd al-Kilā'ī (*Dārimī*).

'Learn them and teach them to your women and children, for they are a blessing, a recitation, and a supplication', reports Abū Dharr (*Ḥākim*).

Surahs al-Baqarah and Āl 'Imrān (*2 and 3*)

'Read the two radiant ones - *al-Baqarah* and *Al 'Imran* - for they will come on the Day of Resurrection like two clouds, or two shades, or two flocks of birds, pleading for their companions', reports Abū Umāmah (*Muslim*).

'The Qur'ān will be brought on the Day of Resurrection, along with its companions who used to act by it, at the front being Surah *al-Baqarah* and *Āl 'Imrān* like two black clouds or canopies with light, or two flocks of birds pleading for their companion', reports al-Nawwās ibn Sam'ān (*Muslim*).

Surah al-Baqarah (2)

'Do not turn your homes into a graveyard [by giving up reading the Qur'ān]. Satan flees from a house in which Surah *al-Baqarah* is recited', reports Abū Hurayrah (*Muslim*).

'Recite Surah *al-Baqarah*: for to hold on to it is a *barakah* (blessing), to leave it is a regret', reports Abū Umāmah (*Muslim*).

'Everything has a hump, and the hump of the Qur'ān is *al-Baqarah'*, reports Abū Hurayrah (*Tirmidhī*).

Surah al-An'ām (6)

'So many Angels accompanied its revelation that the horizon was covered with them', reports Jābir (*Ḥākim*).

Surah al-Kahf (18)

'Whoever learns and preserves, in heart and practice, the first ten Ayahs of *al-Kahf*, he will be protected from *al-Dajjāl'*, reports Abū al-Dardā' (*Muslim*).

'Whoever recites Surah *al-Kahf* on a Friday, light will shine brightly for him till next Friday', reports Abū Sa'īd (*Ḥākim*).

Surah Yā Sīn (36)

'Everything has a heart and the heart of the Qur'ān is *Yā Sīn*. Anyone who reads it, God will write down for him ten readings of the Qur'ān', reports Anas (*Tirmidhī*).

'Whoever reads *Yā Sīn*, seeking Allah's pleasure, his past sins will be forgiven, so recite it over the dying among you', reports Ma'qil ibn Yasār (*Baihaqī*).

Surah al-Fatḥ (48)

'I like it more than anything under the sun', reports 'Umar (*Bukhārī*).

Surah al-Raḥmān (55)

'Everything has an adornment, and the adornment of the Qur'ān is *al-Raḥmān*', reports 'Abdullāh ibn Mas'ūd (*Bayhaqī*).

Surah al-Wāqi'ah (56)

'Whoever recites Surah *al-Wāqi'ah* every night will not go hungry', reports 'Abdullāh ibn Mas'ūd (*Bayhaqī*).

Surah al-Mulk (67)

'This, containing thirty verses, intercedes for a man till his sins are forgiven', reports Abū Hurayrah (*Aḥmad, Tirmidhī, Abū Dā'ūd*).

'I love that it be in the heart of every believer', reports 'Abdullāh ibn 'Abbās (*Ḥākim*).

Surah al-A'lā (87)

'He loved this Surah', reports 'Alī (*Aḥmad*).

Appendix 2

Suggested Syllabuses for Qur'ānic Study

Suggesting a syllabus of Qur'ān passages for study, individually or in study circles, presents formidable difficulties. Firstly, what to include? An adequate or satisfactory selection is almost impossible, short of the whole Qur'ān. Every part of it has something additional or new to say. Even the seemingly repetitive and similar passages have their own insights to offer. A limited number of passages can include only a limited number of themes. Every syllabus will therefore suffer from the serious defect of omitting many more, equally or even more important, themes. Further, any selective approach must be arbitrary, and will reflect only the preferences of the selector, not necessarily of the Qur'ān. These limitations are very important to bear in mind while using the syllabuses suggested here: remain conscious that whatever is omitted is equally valuable and that you are being guided by a fallible human being.

Secondly, where to begin, where to end, and in what order to proceed? The only satisfactory order can be the Qur'ānic order itself, as revealed by Allah. But a syllabus cannot avoid changing that order, so can the order be changed and if so on what criteria? Again, that must be arbitrary. Any order can only be one alternative among many equally useful ones. You may proceed by first establishing the status of the Qur'ān as Divine, and then introducing the evidence in the universe, self and history; faith in Allah, *Ākhirah,* and *Risālah;* individual and collective morality; the goal and purpose of Muslim life; the call to Īmān and Jihad, and fulfilling commitment and pledge to Allah. Or, one may start from the basic faith. What I have preferred here – something which may be changed from situation to situation – is to start by reminding the readers of the blessings of Islam, their goal in life, and their pledge to Allah. This is based on my understanding of how Allah addresses 'Muslims-gone-astray' in al-Baqarah 2: 40-7.

Every circle must begin with a discussion of how to read and understand the Qur'ān. For this purpose the present book should be helpful.

A special word about Surah al-Fātiḥah. It occupies a unique place in the Qur'ān, containing within it the whole world of its essential meanings. You read it many times every day. This should therefore form part of every syllabus. But a novice will need help – a good teacher or *tafsīr* book – to derive the necessary benefit from its study. Wherever such help is available, it *must* be included in the syllabus, even at the cost of dropping one of the suggested passages.

Also of importance are the short Surahs at the end of the Qur'ān which you read in your daily Prayers. Again, you will need help for a proper understanding. They should be studied whenever proper resources are available.

Two syllabuses are given here. The shorter syllabus – of 12 selections – should be useful as a one-year course for study circles, or, for more intensive short duration, say a 12-week or 14-day educational/training course, provided enough time is available for study and preparation, or a teacher is present. It may also be used to devise still shorter, say 5-7 day syllabuses.

With each selection I have given some – and remember only some, not all – major points which you may reflect upon. Some Qur'ānic references are also given so that you may reflect upon them in their light. These references, too, are by no means exhaustive, and their relevance is based on my own understanding. As you proceed less references are given, for it is hoped that you will become more initiated and familiar by then.

The longer syllabus – of 40 selections – is intended as a one-year course for weekly study circles.

The Shorter Syllabus: 12 Selections

One-year course for monthly circles, or short-duration intensive courses.

1. **Surah al-Ḥajj 22: 77-8**

Reflect on: life of worship and obedience; culminating and fulfilled in Jihad; centred on the mission of *Shahādah;* purpose of being Muslim; resources of *Ṣalāh, Zakāh* and *i'tiṣām bi'llāh* (holding fast on to Allah).

1.1 On *rukū'* and *sujūd,* as acts of worship and obedience; representing Prayers, especially during nights; as states of the heart; and attitudes of conduct; in private and public: 2: 125; 16: 49; 2: 43; 76: 26; 39: 9; 77: 48; 5: 55; 96: 19; 9: 112; 48: 29; 2: 58.

1.2 On *'Ibādah,* as the purpose of creation; the central message from Allah; total obedience and surrender; pertaining to the whole of life; turning away from all false gods: 51: 56; 16: 36; 21: 25; 4: 36; 39: 11; 40: 66; 12: 40.

1.3 On *khayr,* extending from the heart to each and every part of life: 8: 70; 2: 269; 2: 180; 73: 20; 99: 7.

1.4 On Jihad, and its due: 49: 15; 8: 74; 3: 142; 9: 19-22; 4: 95-6; 61: 11; 9: 41-5; 9: 24.

1.5 On being chosen for the mission of *Shahādah,* and belonging to Ibrāhīm: 2: 128-9; 2: 143; 6: 161-4; 3: 65-8.

1.6 On Ibrāhīm's *uswah* of *Tawḥīd,* obedience, and sacrifice: 6: 79; 60: 4; 2: 131.

1.7 On *Dīn,* having no hardship: 5: 3-6; 2: 185; 26-8.

1.8 On the mission of *Shahādah:* 2: 213; 33: 45; 5: 67; 48: 8; 3: 187; 4: 41; 2: 159-63, 174-6.

1.9 On *Ṣalāh,* its importance; internal and external conditions for its *iqāmah:* 2: 3; 19: 59; 70: 23, 34; 2: 238; 4: 102-3; 2: 239; 29: 45; 7: 29; 23: 2; 4: 43; 17: 78; 4: 142; 2: 43; 7: 31; 62: 9-11; 19: 55; 107: 1-7; 22: 41.

1.10 On *Zakāh,* its importance and spirit: 41: 6-7; 9: 5; 30: 39; 9: 103.

1.11 On *i'tiṣām bi'llāh*: 3: 101; 31: 22; 26: 77-82.

2. **Surah al-Baqarah 2: 40-7**

Reflect on: remembering the blessing of guidance, and others; fulfilling the pledge to Allah (*'ahd);* renewal of Īmān; bartering away Allah's message for trifling gains; overlaying and distorting truth with falsehood; concealing the truth; *Ṣalāh; Zakāh;* collective life in Prayer; and outside; hypocrisy and duplicity; *ṣabr* and *Ṣalāh* as the moral resources; faith in meeting Allah, when nothing will avail, as their basis.

2.1 On *ni'mah* in guidance; in nature; in history: 5: 3; 2: 150; 5: 7; 16: 18; 3: 103; 8: 26; 5: 20.

2.2 On *'ahd:* 9: 111; 48: 8-10; 7: 172; 36: 60; 33: 21-4; 5: 12-13; 3: 76-7.

2.3 On Allah's part of bargain, in this world and the Hereafter, see additionally: 3: 139; 24: 55; 5: 66; 4: 66-9.

2.4 On summons to the renewal of Īmān: 4: 136-9; 57: 7-16; 4: 60-1.

2.5 On bartering Īmān away for worldly gains: 5: 44; 2: 174-6.

2.6 On overlaying and confounding the truth with falsehood, in beliefs and practices: 2: 75, 78, 79, 80, 85, 91, 94, 102, 111, 113; 5: 18.

2.7 On concealing the truth: 2: 157-63; 174-6.

2.8 On the emphasis on praying, and therefore living wholly, with *Jama'ah;* congregational prayer in *masjid* as the microcosm of Islamic *Jama'ah:* 18: 28; 9: 16-17; 24: 36; 2: 114; 9: 107-8.

2.9 On discrepancy between words and deeds, especially in *da'wah:* 61: 2-3; 63: 1-4.

2.10 On *ṣabr* and *Ṣalāh* as essential resources for fulfilling commitment to Allah: 2: 153-7; 41: 35; 46: 35; 7: 137; 8: 46; 3: 125; 8: 65-6.

2.11 On awareness and certainty of returning to Allah and meeting Allah as the basis of *ṣabr* and *Ṣalāh:* 52: 48.

3. **Surah al-Muzzammil 73: 1-10 and 20**

Reflect on (*i'tiṣām bi'llah* through) Qur'ān reading in night Prayers, *dhikr, tabattul, tawakkul, ṣabr, Ṣalāh, Zakāh; infāq, istighfār.*

3.1 On *qiyāmu 'l-layl:* 32: 15-16; 39: 9-23; 51: 15-19; 17: 78-82.

3.2 On *tasbīḥ* during the day as *da'wah:* 20: 24-33.

3.3 On *dhikr* as the key to *tazkiyyah,* all the time, in varied forms, by heart, tongue, body, deeds, *da'wah,* Jihad: 87: 15; 3: 191; 13: 28; 39: 22-3; 62: 9; 2: 150-5.

3.4 On *tawakkul,* as a key inner resource, based on *Tawḥīd;* its spirit and need: 8: 2-4; 65: 3; 11: 123; 12: 67; 25: 58; 14: 12.

3.5 On various forms of *yaqūlūn,* which require *ṣabr:* 34: 8; 21: 5; 25: 4-5, 7; 68: 8-15; 17: 90-3; 10: 15; 17: 73.

3.6 On *qarḍ ḥasanah,* and spending in the way of Allah (*infāq*): 57: 11-16; 92: 18-21; 23: 60; 2: 264-74; 3: 92; 4: 38; 57: 10; 63: 11; 35: 29.

3.7 On *istighfār* as central to Allah's message, watching, scrutiny, accountability, regretting, turning back, rewards in this-world and that-world: 4: 110; 3: 15-17; 3: 133-6; 3: 146-8; 71: 7-12; 39: 53; 64: 17.

4. **Surah al-Ḥadīd 57: 1-7**

Reflect on: everything glorifying Allah; to Him belongs kingship; power to give life and death; power over everything; knowledge of everything; sovereignty and rule; over time; knowledge of what lies in hearts; summons to Īmān and *infāq* in this context.

4.1 On Allah's attributes: 22: 18; 17: 44; 10: 31-6; 6: 59-61; 3: 154; 28: 70-2; 2: 255; 59: 22-4; 3: 25-6.

5. **Surah al-Naḥl 16: 1-22**

Reflect on: evidence in the universe and self for *Tawḥīd, Ākhirah* and *Risālah:* purposeful creation; of heavens and earth; of man; of animals; sending down of water; growing of crops; night and day; sun, moon and stars; diversity in colours; food and wealth from oceans; guidance through stars.

5.1 On evidence, in similar passages: 30: 17-27; 27: 59-68; 10: 1-10, 31-6.

6. **Surah Yā Sīn 36: 50-65**

Reflect on various stages of journey beyond life: coming of death and the last hour; resurrection; reckoning; judgement; reward; punishment.

6.1 On *Ākhirah:* 50: 16-35; *75:* 20-30; 18: 47-9; 20: 100-12; 22: 1-7; 23: 99-118; 43: 66-80; 44: 40-59; 51: 1-27.

7. **Surah al-Hadīd 57: 20-5**

Reflect on: nature and the reality of present life; preparedness to give life and money; for helping Allah and His Messenger; through power; employed to establish justice among men.

7.1 On the present life and the life to come: 3: 14-15, 185; 10: 24; 18: 45; 4: 134; 17: 18-19; 42: 19-20.

7.2 On establishing justice and equity: 4: 135; 61: 9-14.

8. **Surah al-'Ankabūt 28: 1-10**

Reflect on: the essentiality of trials and tribulations to test Īmān, and to bring success.

8.1 See 2: 155; 2: 214; 3: 140-2, 179; 47: 29-31.

9. **Surah al-Anfāl 8: 72-5**

Reflect on the inherent and crucial link between Īmān and Hijrah, Jihad, and helping Allah's cause; essentiality of collectivity for Jihad.

10. **Surah al-Tawbah 9: 19-24**

Reflect on: Īmān and Jihad, together, as the highest acts; and sacrificing everything - relatives, wealth, career and business, houses - for the love of Allah, His Messenger, and Jihad in His way.

11. **Surah al-Nūr 24: 47-52 and 62-4**

Reflect on: obedience and response to the Messenger as the basis of collective life established to fulfil Allah's mission.

11.1 See 8: 20-8; 49: 1-5; 58: 11-13; 9: 42-57, 62-6, 81-2; 62: 9-11.

12. **Surah Āl 'Imrān 3: 190-200**

A comprehensive summary: evidence for Allah, *Ākhirah* and *Risālah* in the creation of heavens and earth and alternation of day and night; living a life ever-remembering Allah; Hereafter is the goal; trust and faith in the Messenger; the implications of faith - struggle and tribulations; guidelines for collective life.

It has been assumed that the above syllabus will be studied as part of a larger course, and hence nothing is included on the individual and collective attributes of a Muslim's life. If not, then it would be useful to take up additionally (a) *al-Isrā' 17:* 23-39 (in conjunction with *al-Furqān* 25: 63-77 and *Luqmān* 31: 12-19) and (b) *al-Ḥujurāt 49: 10-14.*

The Longer Syllabus: 40 Selections

One-year course for weekly study circles

1.	*al-Ḥajj 22: 77-8*	Life of worship; Jihad, mission of *Shahadah.*
2.	*al-Tawbah 9: 111-12*	Pledge of Īmān, life of worship.
3.	*al-Nisā' 4: 131-7*	Witnessing to justice, summons to Īmān.
4.	*Āl 'Imrān 3: 102-10*	Purpose of Ummah.
5.	*al-Fatḥ 48: 8-11*	Pledge to continue the Prophet's mission.
6.	*al-Baqarah 2: 40-6*	Call to fulfil the pledge.
7.	*al-Muzzammil* 73: *1-10,20*	Building a relationship with Allah.
8.	*al-Isrā' 17: 23-39*	Individual and collective morality.
9.	*al-Naḥl 16: 1-11*	Evidence for *Tawḥīd, Risālah, Ākhirah.*
10.	*al-Naḥl 16: 12-22*	Evidence for *Tawḥīd, Risālah, Ākhirah.*
11.	*Yunūs 10: 31-6*	Evidence for *Tawḥīd,* guidance.
12.	*al-Ḥajj 22: 1-7*	Evidence for *Ākhirah.*
13.	*Qāf 50: 1-18*	Evidence for *Ākhirah.*
14.	*al-Mu'minūn 23: 99-118*	*Ākhirah.*
15.	*Yā Sīn 36: 50-65*	*Ākhirah.*

16.	*Qāf 50: 19-35*	*Ākhirah.*
17.	*al-Zumar 39: 53-66*	Preparing for *Ākhirah.*
18.	*al-Ḥashr 59: 18-24*	Preparing for *Ākhirah,* Allah's attributes.
19.	*al-Ḥadīd 57: 1-7*	Allah's attributes; summons to Īmān and *infāq.*
20.	*al-Ḥadīd 57: 12-17*	Īmān and *infāq.*
21.	*al-Ḥadīd 57: 20-5*	Present life; *infāq,* establishing justice.
22.	*al-Ṣaff 61: 9-14*	Call to commit to the Prophet's mission, Īmān, Jihad
23.	*al-'Ankabūt 29:1-11*	Testing of faith.
24.	*al-Anfāl 8: 72-5*	Īmān, Hijrah, Jihad, *Jamā'ah.*
25.	*al-Nisā' 4: 95-100*	Hijrah, Jihad.
26.	*al-Tawbah 9: 19-24*	Jihad, the highest act; sacrificing everything.
27.	*al-Tawbah 9: 38-45*	Jihad.
28.	*Āl 'Imrān 3: 169-75*	Dying in the way of Allah.
29.	*al-Baqarah 2: 261-6*	*Infāq fi Sabīli'llāh.*
30.	*al-Baqarah 2: 267-72*	*Infāq fi Sabīli'llāh.*
31.	*al-Anfāl 8: 20-9*	Collective life, obedience.
32.	*al-Nisā' 4: 60-7*	Collective life, obedience.
33.	*al-Nūr 24: 47-52,62-4*	Collective life: response and obedience.
34.	*al-Ḥujurāt 49: 1-9*	Collective life: relationship with leaders.

35.	*al-Mujādalah 58: 7-13*	Collective life: rules and duties.
36.	*al-Ḥujurāt 49: 10-15*	Collective life: interpersonal relations.
37.	*Fuṣṣilat 41: 30-6*	Da'wah and required attributes.
38.	*al-Baqarah 2: 150-63*	Mission and its obligations.
39.	*Āl 'Imrān 3:185-92*	Summary.
40.	*Āl 'Imrān 3: 193-200*	Summary.

Only 40 selections have been given for 52 weeks, allowing for the fact that some weeks will have to be taken off and some selections may take more than a week to study.

However, if time is available, it may be devoted to the study of passages on history in the Qur'ān – a theme which I have not included here. In this respect I would suggest taking up one prophet each week, such as Nūḥ or Hūd, basing the study on one passage in Surah al-A'rāf, but also referring to other relevant places in the Qur'ān.

1. *al-A'rāf* 7: *59-64*
2. *al-A'rāf 7:* 65-72
3. *al-A'rāf 7:* 73-9
4. *al-A'rāf 7:* 80-4
5. *al-A'rāf 7:* 85-93
6. *al-A'rāf* 7: *94-102*
7. *Hūd 11: 116-23.*

Appendix 3

Aids to Study

Translations

No translation can perhaps ever be satisfactory, nor is an authorized or standard version possible. You may use any of the following. Those by Yusuf Ali and Muhammad Asad provide short explanatory notes too, some of which are quite valuable.

Towards Understanding the Qur'ān: Abridged Version, by Sayyid Abul A'lā Mawdūdī.

The Holy Qur'ān: Text, Translation and Commentary, by Abdullah Yusuf Ali.

The Message of the Qur'ān, translated and explained by Muhammad Asad.

The Koran Interpreted, by Arthur J. Arberry.

Commentaries

No really good commentary of the full Qur'ān is available in the English language which can be unhesitatingly recommended to a beginner. The following may be found useful, in addition to some partial commentaries like those by Sayyid Qutb, Abul Kalam Azad, which are not listed here but may provide some insights.

Towards Understanding the Qur'ān, by Sayyid Abul A'lā Mawdūdī, 9 vols up to Sūrah 37.

In the Shade of the Qur'ān, by Sayyid Quṭb, 18 vols (complete).

Tafsirul Qur'ān: Translation and Commentary, Vols. I-III (complete), by Abdul Majid Daryabadi.

Dictionaries

Arabic-English Lexicon, by E. W. Lane, based on by far the best Arabic dictionary, *Lisān al-'Arab,* should be of great help.

Arabic-English Dictionary of Qur'ānic Usage, by Elsaid M. Badawi and Muhammad Abdel Haleem.

Concordances

Al-Mu'jam al-Mufahras li Alfāẓ al-Qur'ān al-Karīm, by Muhammad Fu'ād al-Bāqī.

A Concordance of the Qur'ān, by Hanna E. Kassis.

You can locate any part of the Qur'ān if you remember just one word, but you should have the ability to find the root of that word.

'Ulūm al-Qur'ān

'Ulūm al-Qur'ān: An Introduction to the Sciences of the Qur'ān by Ahmad von Denffer.

Etiquette with the Qur'ān, by Imam al-Nawawi.

Study Guides

The Qur'ān: Basic Teachings, by T.B. Irving, K. Ahmad and M. M. Ahsan.

Qur'ānic Keywords, by Abdur Rashid Siddiqui.

Index

THE QUR'ĀNIC VERSES